To Lassie & Keanu

ALSO BY PATRICIA B. McCONNELL

BOOKS

For the Love of a Dog:
Understanding Emotions in You and Your Best Friend

The Other End of the Leash:
Why We Do What We Do Around Dogs

BOOKLETS

How to be Leader of the Pack
And Have Your Dog Love You for it!

The Cautious Canine:
How to Help Dogs Conquer Their Fears

I'll Be Home Soon!
How to Prevent and Treat Separation Anxiety

The Fastidious Feline:
How to Prevent and Treat Litter Box Problems

Way to Go!
How to Housetrain a Dog of Any Age
(by Karen B. London and Patricia B. McConnell)

Feeling Outnumbered?
How to Manage and Enjoy Your Multi-Dog Household
(by Karen B. London and Patricia B. McConnell)
Available as both booklet and DVD

Feisty Fido
Help for the Leash Aggressive Dog
(by Patricia B. McConnell and Karen B. London)

Lassie Come! DVD
How to get your dog to come every time you call!

Family Friendly
Dog Training

Patricia B. McConnell, Ph.D.
and Aimee Moore

Dog's Best Friend, Ltd. Black Earth, WI

Cover photograph by C&N Photography.
Cover and internal design by jam graphics & design.

ISBN # 1-891767-11-9
For information, contact:
www.dogsbestfriendtraining.com
or
PHONE 608 767-2435   FAX 608 767-5802

Printed in the United States of America

9 8 7 6 5 4 3 2 1
First Edition

CONTENTS

INTRODUCTION

"Lassie! Run down to the barn and get Timmy! Not the small barn, the big one on the north side! And hurry—there's a storm coming!"

If you aren't old enough to remember watching Lassie the wonder dog on television, you've at least heard of her—the beautiful Rough-coated Collie who did everything she was asked, seemingly without any training whatsoever. Lassie always came when called, never jumped up on Aunt Polly, and never had an accident in the house. Ah, Lassie—if only all dogs arrived just like her: automatically understanding English, able to read our minds, and most importantly, always willing to do what we ask, simply because we ask it.

LASSIE WAS AN ACTOR As we all know, Lassie wasn't really a family pet, and her behavior can't be compared to that of our own dogs. The shiny-eyed, four-legged fuzzballs at our feet didn't come with software programs that guarantee obedience, nor did they come with a television director who could make any dog look like a star. We may think of dogs as members of our family, but they aren't short, furry people and they often have no understanding of what we want. Besides, even if they were furry people—how many people do you know who do everything you ask?!

Think of our expectations on dogs from their perspective: Walk quietly down the sidewalk shoulder-to-shoulder with my human? *What? We dogs don't walk together like that, that's just silly.* Ignore a squirrel who dashes across the trail in front of me? *Why on earth would I do that?* Sit down when visitors come to the door? *How rude! Polite dogs greet one another by licking another's mouth, so a good dog should jump up to kiss those inconveniently placed muzzles looming high above us.*

Because dogs don't inherently understand the rules of human societies, and because we expect so much of them, it is up to us to teach them manners, to do what we ask when we ask it, and most importantly, that it's fun to pay attention to us. If you have a dog, that's a good summary of your job description: helping your dog understand what you expect of him, and doing it in such a way that it's fun and rewarding for both of you.

And that brings up the animal at the other end of the leash—you. You didn't come pre-programmed either, and there's no reason you should know how to train dogs just because you love them. If you're a novice, training a dog is a bit like getting on an untrained horse, having never ridden yourself. No wonder things don't always go smoothly. You weren't born knowing how to train a dog anymore than you were born knowing how to play basketball, so don't be hard on yourself if, at times, the learning curve feels a bit steep. Just like a new sport, dog training takes knowledge, practice and a good coach.

The good news is that dog training isn't rocket science, and just a little bit of practice can go a long way toward creating a joyful, loving relationship with your dog. Happy, well-mannered dogs have owners who are clear and consistent and who use patience and knowledge to teach dogs to behave. The goal of this book is to teach dog lovers how to combine humane, effective training methods with an understanding of dog behavior to create dogs who listen and respond, even when a squirrel dashes across their path. The chapters that follow will help you teach your dog the basics, like sit, lie down, coming when called, and staying when asked, but we hope they do more than that. Our ultimate goal is to help you expand your ability to connect with your best friend in a way that will enrich your relationship for years to come.

This manual is structured around six weeks of training, and is designed to either accompany training classes or to be used on its own. Each chapter follows one week of training, and includes a topic of general interest at the beginning and each week's exercises at the end. The book is designed for you to read one chapter a week, and work on the exercises within it one week at a time. However, don't hesitate to use it in any way you choose—you could read all the general topics in one sitting, or just follow through with one exercise, like coming when called, week to week. Of course, your dog won't be fully trained after just six weeks, but you'll have the tools you need to continue working on the exercises that are important to you. Whether you're involved in a class or home schooling, you'll get the most out of this book if you practice the exercises in short sessions scattered throughout the day, be sure to give your dog lots and lots of treats and praise for doing the right thing (especially early in training), and always be aware of whether your dog is capable of doing what you ask. You'll have a much better behaved dog in the long run if you set her up to "win," rather than creating situations in which she'll fail and become frustrated. Of course, no book can cover everything there is to know about dog training and behavior, but Aimee and I have done our best to summarize what we think is most important, in a format accessible for people who love their dogs—but who can't quit their day jobs and become professional trainers.

So congratulations—by picking up this training manual, you and your dog are embarking on a journey together, an adventure we hope will bring happiness to both of you for many years to come.

1

GOOD DOG!

THE POSITIVES OF POSITIVE REINFORCEMENT Twelve years ago I agreed to foster a year-old Border Collie for a couple of weeks. She arrived late one night, and early the next morning I let her out with the other dogs, who dashed up the hill after a squirrel. I don't know what I was thinking when I called out her name as she ran, flat out, after the other dogs, but when I did she turned in mid-air and hit the ground running toward me. She flipped her neat little body at my feet and sat shoulder to shoulder with me, looked up at my face and grinned. No wonder I decided then and there to keep her—a dog who comes when called, with no training whatsoever? Wow. I changed her name to Lassie, appropriately enough. She's sleeping at my feet as I write this, and at thirteen years of age, she's still one of the best things that ever happened to me.

However, my Lassie also needed to be house trained, to learn to chew on dog toys instead of sweaters, and to stop leaping onto visitor's shoulders at the door. She arrived with a set of obsessive-compulsive disorders, a fear of unfamiliar men and an expert version of "catch me if you can when I have a dish towel in my mouth."

As wonderful as she was, my Lassie still needed lots of training, and she needed me to provide it. Without training, Lassie would have looked more like Marmaduke than her namesake on television. Now she's a model citizen, because I used a type of training that was great fun for both of us. This training is called *positive reinforcement*, and it teaches dogs, kindly and gently, that it is worthwhile to do what you ask. The basics are simple: dogs learn that good things happen if they sit on cue or come when called, and so they want to do it again.

Positive reinforcements—like treats, games of fetch, or chest rubs— are things that cause your dog to want to repeat an action, whether it is sitting when visitors come to the front door or walking beside you on a leash.

Positive reinforcement has many advantages.[1] It makes training fun for everyone, both trainer and trainee. That's not a trivial advantage: the more fun it is, the more you'll do it and the better your dog will behave. Rather than teaching your dog to be afraid of you, as often happens with force-based training, your dog will learn that you're fun and fair and can be counted on to be her best friend—even if you do have only two legs and have lost most of your fur. Positive reinforcement is a great way to teach your dog to listen to you, without creating a spoiled dog who does whatever she wants, whenever she wants.[2]

Positive reinforcement is the most user-friendly of all training techniques. Although *great* dog training takes a lot of knowledge and skill, *good* dog training takes a basic understanding of how to use reinforcements, a bit of knowledge about how dogs see the world, and the desire to create a healthy and happy relationship with your dog. If you'll supply the desire, we'll supply the rest. By the end of this program—in just six short weeks—you'll be well on your way to being best friends with a polite and happy dog.

DOGS KNOW BEST There are a few keys to using positive reinforcement correctly. One is to remember that it's your dog who defines what is reinforcing, not you. The good-looking treats you bought at the market may say that all dogs love them, but your dog might not have read the label. You may think your dog loves it when you pat-pat him on the head, but many dogs aren't enamored with that type of petting. The good news is that you can count on your dog to tell you what he loves—just go out of your way to pay attention to his reaction when you reinforce him. That sounds obvious, but a common mistake of novice dog trainers is not noticing their dog's lackluster response, so watch your dog carefully when you're treating or petting

A key to using positive reinforcement correctly is to remember that it's your dog who defines what is reinforcing, not you.

[1] In the interest of simplicity, for the rest of the book we'll use reinforcement as a synonym of positive reinforcement.
[2] Note to reader: rather than using "he" or "she" exclusively, or using the awkward "he or she" when referring to a dog, the text alternates between referring to a dog as "he" or "she" throughout the book. It's simpler that way—and in dog training, simple is almost always good.

him. If he averts his head or walks away, he probably isn't thrilled about what you're doing. If he stays close and begs for more, then bingo, you've found something he is willing to work for in the future.

IT'S ALL IN THE TIMING Another important aspect of using positive reinforcement is timing. Reinforcements should occur immediately after the action you want your dog to perform. If you ask your dog to sit and he does, he should get something that makes him happy within half of a second of his movement. We humans tend to stand and stare at our dogs for a second or two after they do something we ask, and if dogs could talk, I suspect they'd say it drives them crazy. "Why are they staring at me? Should I have done something else? Wasn't I supposed to sit?" Remember, your dog is always searching for answers from you, and it's up to you to provide them with clear and well-timed responses. Train yourself to deliver a treat instantly after your dog responds, and you'll be amazed at how fast your dog can learn something new.

SECONDARY VS PRIMARY REINFORCEMENT It's worth taking a minute here to talk about two different kinds of reinforcement. Things like food and chase games are called "primary reinforcers," because they inherently make your dog feel good. Pavlov didn't have to condition dogs to drool when he brought meat into the laboratory, and you don't have to teach your dog to be happy when you give him a piece of chicken. Other things we do for our dogs are called "secondary reinforcers," because they have to be linked to something else to be effective. Praise is a perfect example of a secondary reinforcer, because many of our dogs have to learn to feel good when we say nice things to them. It makes sense if you think about it. Why would random noises coming out of your mouth automatically make your dog happy? You may feel good when you say "good girl!," but your dog might not. We all want our dogs to melt into puddles when we praise them, but pretty words all by themselves often aren't enough to make that happen.

It's easy to condition your dog to be happy when you praise him. First, choose your praise word and use it consistently. You could say "Good!" or "Good Boy!" or "Yes!" but get in the habit of using the same word, said in the same way, each time. (We'll use "Good!" throughout the book, but you should choose what you like best.) Several times a day, say your praise word and immediately pop a treat in your dog's mouth.

Reinforcements should occur immediately after the action you want your dog to perform.

Try this in short sessions of 5 to 10 repetitions each, two to three times a day for a couple of days. You can also use your praise word when you're rubbing his belly, when he's eating his dinner, or any other time you're sure he's about to be a happy guy. In just a few days you'll have a dog who loves hearing you say "Good!" and you can use that to help him want to listen to you.

Another popular use of a secondary reinforcer is called "clicker training." This method utilizes a sound from a handheld clicker that functions as a particularly precise and attention-getting substitute for verbal praise. Some people use clickers for all training, others use them for special types of training—tricks and games for example. Whichever method you use, the idea is to link your voice or the clicker to something that your dog loves, so that the sound itself makes the dog feel good when he hears it.

A WORD ABOUT TREATS

WILL WORK FOR FOOD Food is a wonderful way to get a dog's attention, and it's also a great way to reinforce her for doing what you ask. There are several reasons for that: food not only tastes good, it smells good too, and good smells are tightly linked to good emotions in your dog's brain. The other reason food is such a great reinforcement is that you can cut it up into small pieces, put it in your pocket or training pouch and use it repeatedly within one training session.

Keep in mind that your dog gets to define what a "good" treat is. Most dogs like strong-smelling things that smell like meat or cheese. Those kinds of treats are usually enough to compete with distractions in the environment, whereas many commercial treats found in supermarkets are primarily made out of dried wheat or corn (that's grass to a dog!) and just aren't as competitive. Every dog trainer sees hundreds of dogs who "won't work for treats," until the trainer pulls out her own treats and has the dog turning somersaults to get at them. However, some dogs don't read the books, and prefer sweet potatoes to cheese. My dog Pip will do just about anything for a string bean, so take the time to experiment and learn what is a "high-value" versus a "low-value" treat to your own dog.

SHE IS WHAT SHE EATS In the early stages of training, you'll be giving your dog quite a few treats, so keep the pieces very small; about pea size for a medium-sized dog. If you're doing a lot of training (good for you!), you will want to adjust your dog's feeding accordingly. Be sure what you're giving your dog is good for her. There are lots of healthy commercial treats available, found mostly in pet stores, and less often in supermarkets. Read the labels and look for whole, natural ingredients, for example, "chicken" versus "chicken by-products." You can also make your own; lots of professional trainers cut up string cheese, chicken or microwave liver to save on expenses. You can even create your own "trail mix" of different types of food, using the best ones for stellar performances. Again, remember that every dog is different, so experiment and find out what makes your dog happiest, and use that in distracting environments or for new exercises.

NO THANKS Ah, but what about those dogs who aren't interested in food, even if it's filet mignon? There aren't many dogs who fit that description, so if your dog refuses a treat, ask yourself if she's stressed, overly excited, or if she's not motivated by the type of treats you are using. However, there are some dogs who are never motivated by food, no matter where they are or what type of treat you are using. If your dog truly doesn't care about food, no matter how good, you'll need to find something that she *does* love, and use that as a reinforcement. Even if your dog loves food, you'd be wise to vary what you give her, substituting play and exuberant praise on occasion. Lots of dogs love to play ball, and ball play is a wonderful way of reinforcing attention or other appropriate responses. Some dogs aren't interested in playing fetch, but love nothing better than playing with a squeaky toy. Tug of war can be a great reward for some dogs as long as it doesn't cause the dog to become overly aroused. Some hunting dogs will ignore food and toys, but will whip their heads around as if on a string if you pull a bird wing out of your pocket (don't laugh, they're available through hunting supply stores and catalogs!).

Be creative with your reinforcements!

Be creative with your reinforcements: a used Kleenex worked wonders for one trainer, when she found herself without treats or toys, and spontaneously gave it to a dog who did a spectacular recall. I even taught a Gordon Setter to pay attention by picking up a tiny pellet of dried sheep manure and popping it into his mouth.[3] I'm not going to start manufacturing a new line of dog treats in the near future ("Poop Berries! Give your dog what he really wants!"), but you get the idea—your dog knows what he wants, and it's your job to figure it out and use it to your advantage.

WHEN CAN I STOP USING FOOD? The primary concern most people have about using treats is that they'll have to carry around a refrigerator full of treats to get their dog to behave. However, the beauty of using reinforcements is that you can drop them out of your repertoire as your dog's good behavior becomes habitual. After all, no one tells you what a good girl or boy you are for saying "please" and "thank you," right? But you still do it, because it's become such a habit you don't even think about it. That's the same progression you see in dog training—once you establish good habits you won't need to use treats anymore. We haven't given our dogs a treat for a simple sit in years. Of course, we still often thank them ("Good!"), but we don't need to carry food with us unless we're training something new. We'll talk more in later chapters about when you can start to decrease the frequency of treats, but at this stage of training it is essential to use positive reinforcements liberally for any new exercises or any training in distracting environments.

So, with these thoughts in mind, it's time to start working on some exercises. First things first: what could be more important than your dog knowing his name?

The beauty of using positive reinforcements is that you can gradually drop them out of your repertoire as your dog's good behavior becomes habitual.

THIS WEEK'S EXERCISES

THE NAME GAME

A DOG BY ANY OTHER NAME . . . One of the most useful things you can do this week is to be thoughtful about how you use your dog's name. Start by asking yourself how people use names. If you say a person's name, it's because you want her attention, right? Once she gives you her attention, you don't stand and stare at her, you ask her a question or tell her something you think she needs to know. That's how we should use our dogs' names—to get their attention, and then once we have it, we need to do something with it.

[3] Hey, it's just re-cycled grass!

Keep in mind that there's no reason your dog should automatically take her attention off an interesting smell in the grass just because you made a sound that we label a "name." Until we teach them differently, words that have inherent meaning to us are just noises to our dogs. You can make your dog's name meaningful to her by playing what we call the name game. It's some of the easiest training you'll ever do, but it is powerful stuff that can make a big difference in your relationship with your dog. Start by having at least 15 to 25 extra tasty treats in your hand or training pouch, and move into an area in which your dog will be only mildly distracted. Wait for her to start sniffing the grass or looking elsewhere, and then say her name. If she turns her head toward you, immediately say "Good!" and give her a treat. Then turn and look away, perhaps walk a few feet forward, and wait for her to turn her attention elsewhere. When she does, say her name again, praise the instant her head turns toward you and give her another treat. Repeat that four or five times in a row, giving her more than one treat for responding if she was especially interested in something in the environment.

If you say her name and she doesn't turn her head, walk forward a few steps away from what's distracting her, and try again. Once you've said her name, let her initiate the action without any prompting from you. If she initiates looking at you on her own she'll learn faster and be more consistent later on. If you absolutely have to, clap your hands or make smoochy noises to help direct her attention toward you, but after a few repetitions, wait to see if she'll do it on her own, and be lightening fast with the treat to reward her for it.

A cautionary note: just about every human ever born tends to repeat the dog's name if it didn't work the first time. Thus, a reasonable subtitle of this section could be: "Ginger, Ginger, GINGER!" But if you respond to inattention by repeating your dog's name, you're just teaching her to ignore you until the second or third repetition. This week, concentrate on saying your dog's name just once, and then moving to a new spot if it didn't work the first time. Palm the treat in your hand and let her sniff your fist to get her attention, and then pull your hand back and let her turn her head away before you try again. If you're not getting a good response, try working in a less distracting environment. Play this game several times a day, varying when and where you ask her to look

Until we teach them differently, the words that have inherent meaning to us are just noises to our dogs.

at you. Be mindful of the level of difficulty—don't get swept away by early successes and ask for her to turn away from high-level distractions yet. You always want to build on a foundation of success, so be sure to go one step at a time.

Along with playing the name game, notice how and when you say your dog's name. Many of us (okay, all of us!) tend to say our dog's name often, but not necessarily in a way that is useful. Often we say "Fido" or "Laddie," and assume that through some miraculous process our dogs will know that what we really meant was "Fido come!" or "Lad, don't chew on the electric cord." But alas, mind-reading dogs have yet to be bred, and until that happens we need to go out of our way to ensure that we are effectively communicating. Don't worry when you notice yourself saying your dog's name and nothing else, but make a mental note of it. After a few days, without consciously trying, you'll start making yourself worth listening to, and your dog will magically become better behaved!

TEACHING DOGS TO SIT ON CUE

LURE AND REWARD We teach dogs to sit on cue with what's called the "lure and reward" method, first popularized by veterinary behaviorist Ian Dunbar. With this technique you *lure* your dog into the position you want with the smell of a tasty treat in your hand, and then *reward* him by letting him eat it. There are several advantages to using this method: first, by luring the dog into the correct position, you're communicating to him what it is you want him to do. When done correctly, it allows you to make rapid progress in just one session, and gives you a chance to use lots of reinforcement to motivate him to sit when asked. Second, by luring the dog into a sitting position, you are creating a foundation to teach both a visual and a verbal cue. It's very handy to be able to communicate both ways to your dog—Aimee and I use both voice and movement on a daily basis with our own dogs, and our clients appreciate being able to use hand signals while they're on the phone or too far away for their dog to hear them. Visual cues are especially valuable because dogs naturally respond to them better than they do to sounds—in spite of all that barking, most social signals between dogs are visual, so dogs come hard-wired to pay attention to our movements.

The first step in teaching your dog to come on cue is to decide what cue you're going to use, and use it consistently.

Even if your dog already knows to sit when asked, it's handy to practice teaching sit with the lure and reward method. It's a great way to teach both a verbal and a visual cue, and you'll have learned a practical and useful method of teaching him other things later on. To get started, put a tasty, smelly treat in your hand, and move it to within an inch or two of your dog's nose. Let him smell the hidden treat to get his attention focused on your hand, and then move your hand slowly backward, through his ears, toward his tail. Don't raise your hand up in the air, or you'll just teach him to leap up to get the treat. Keep your hand only an inch or so above his head as you move the treat through his ears, and toward his tail. If he keeps his eyes on your hand, his chin will raise up and his hindquarters will plop down. As soon as that happens, say "Good!" and immediately give him the treat. If your dog won't sit down as you lure the treat toward his tail, try moving him so that he's facing out of a corner, and can't back up without hitting a wall. Notice that you haven't said "sit" yet. Hold off on using the cue until you can reliably get him to sit by moving your hand over his head toward his tail. Once you're willing to bet ten dollars that he'll do it the next time, say "sit" a split second before you start moving your hand.

As with all new exercises, practice this in a quiet, non-distracting environment. You'll be most successful if you scatter your training sessions throughout the day, and keep each session short. Most dogs do best if asked to sit no more than five to six times in a row, and for some smart dogs, even that may be too much. When you're practicing, vary the location, and how often you ask him to sit in one session. Try asking for a sit just once, at least two or three times a day. As long as he sits as asked, give him the treat, celebrate his brilliance and go on to something else. If he didn't do so well, continue until he improves, and then stop on a good note.

After a few days of practice, start to focus on the movement of your hand. Notice that your hand is moving in an upward curve as you lure your dog—it's that movement that will evolve into your visual cue. Begin to emphasize the upward sweep of your hand, moving it less over his head and toward his tail, and more in an upward curve toward your body. Dogs seem to learn this visual cue remarkably easily (more easily than your vocal cue), and it'll come in handy when you're on the phone, company is walking in the door and your kids are calling to you from the other room.

COMING WHEN CALLED

WELL WORTH THE EFFORT One of the most valuable things you can teach your dog is to come when called. Ironically, the more control you have over your dog, the more freedom your dog can have, so the time you spend on this exercise is well worth it. If your dog comes running on cue, you can call him in from the backyard when you're late for work, away from a potential fight at the dog park, and back to you when he spots a deer in the woods. That means you can take him on walks in the woods and let him play at the dog park with his buddies. Surely teaching a dog to come when called is as important to his happiness as it is to yours.

Ironically, the more control you have over your dog, the more freedom your dog can have.

The first step in teaching your dog to come on cue is to decide what cue you're going to use, and to use it consistently. This sounds easy, but it turns out to be a challenge to us humans, who love to do the equivalent of jazz riffs on the words we use. "Chester, come!" is often followed by "come, Chester" and "Chester, over here!" and "C'mon, hurry up" (along with other terms best left unwritten). Having a rich and varied vocabulary is a great benefit in science and literature, but it turns out to be a problem in dog training. If you want your dog to come consistently, then you need to be consistent yourself. Remember, your dog didn't come speaking English—don't confuse him by using different sounds for the same cue. So, right now, before you go any further, decide as a family exactly what your come cue is going to be, and use it, and it alone, during training. The best cues are short, punchy kinds of sounds like "Drift! come!" or "Pup! Pup! Pup!" Hand claps work especially well: in my research on acoustics and canine responses, I found that hand claps were the most successful of ten different sounds (like claps, words and whistles) to get puppies to run to the sound source.

How you position your body is also going to have a big effect on your dog's behavior. Your dog is more likely to stay away if you stand squarely facing him and step forward as you call "come." Your voice may be saying "come," but to a dog, your body is communicating a warning to not come any closer, as if you were a traffic cop stopping oncoming cars. Dogs want to go in the direction that your feet are going, so when you call your dog to come, turn your body sideways, and move away from your dog as you call. Your movement away from him will draw your dog toward you, rather than blocking him from moving forward.[4] You'll have to concentrate on this at first; it's not natural to turn your body and move away from your dog as you call him to come. That's an understatement—sometimes trainers have to take people by the sleeve and pull them away from their dogs—but making this one change often results in miraculously better-behaved dogs, so take it to heart.

THE COME GAME In the first phase of teaching come, turn your training sessions into playful romps, in which your dog learns that running to you when called is the best game in town. From no more than six to ten feet away, call out your dog's come cue (create a new one if you've used one that your dog has learned to ignore!), turn your body sideways, start clapping and running away from your dog. As soon as he moves even a few inches in your direction, sing out "Good Boy!" and keep going. When he catches up to you, Yeee haw—have a party! Give him an extra tasty treat, praise him to the skies and if he likes it, give him some great rubs on his chest or rump.

Keep in mind that the hardest part of a recall is when your dog has to turn his attention off what he's doing and onto you. That's why you should sing out "Good!" with enthusiasm the instant he turns his head and starts moving toward you—he needs reinforcing long before he arrives at your feet. Here's where you get to reap the rewards of linking praise with a food treat. Because he's learned that praise leads to food, he'll be reinforced when he needs to be, right after he begins doing what you want him to do. When he arrives, you can pop a tasty treat in his mouth and praise him some more.[5] Now he's been reinforced twice: once with your praise for shifting his attention onto you, and again with food and praise for arriving at your feet. A word to the wise: most people don't praise their dog soon enough, so consciously force yourself to say the word(s) as fast as you can after your dog turns toward you. This is a great time to practice your timing as a trainer—see if you can say "good" before he takes a second stride in your direction.

---

[4] This tip is described at length in The Other End of the Leash, and has received more grateful comments than any other part of the book. Several people have written that they are sure it saved their dog's life, so take this advice to seriously.

[5] This isn't the time to ask for a sit, because then he'll think the treat is for sitting, not coming when called.

Come training is also a great example of the importance of being sure about what your dog loves and what you just think he loves. For example, in every one of our beginning family dog training classes you can watch owners pat-patting the top of their dogs' heads, believing that they are reinforcing their dogs for coming.[6] However, if you watch for it, you can see the dogs turning their heads away in a canine version of "yuck." Remember, you're trying to condition your dog to feel good when he runs toward you on cue, so you must be sure that your dog is really happy that he came when called (just like Pavlov conditioned his dogs to drool to the sound of a bell). Watch your dog's immediate response to your praise, petting or treats: does he stay with you, wagging from the shoulders back? Great, then your praise and treats were true reinforcements. Does he turn his head and walk away? Whoops, time to rethink what you're doing to make him glad he came.

WHEN AND WHERE Repeat this game several times a day in short sessions, conditioning your dog to link the cue "come" with running toward you and feeling good about it. Be sure to scatter these sessions throughout the day, playing the game in different areas of your home. You'll want to call him to come to you at least 10 or 20 times a day during early training. That may seem like a lot, but if you do a little here and a little there it will be easy. You can also opportunistically call him to come when you know he'll run to you anyway: for example when you get out his dinner bowl or when he runs to greet you.

Be thoughtful about when you call your dog to come.

Be thoughtful about *when* you call your dog to come. At this stage, avoid calling your dog to come if he's intensely focused on something else. Your goal is to create a foundation of coming *every* time he's called, so don't set your dog up to fail (and to learn to ignore you when he feels like it). If you eventually want a dog to come away from a vigorous play session at the dog park, then you need to start with him coming every time he's called and being really glad he did.

This sounds simple, but it turns out to be one of the greatest challenges for novice dog owners. It's tempting to call a dog to come without

[6] A note to readers about the term owner: the word "owner" might not be the best term to describe who we are to our dogs, but it's used throughout the book in the sense of "Lassie is my dog, and I am her human." The term "guardian" is becoming increasingly popular, but, perhaps being too old and set in my ways, it seems formal and lawyerly to me. In reality, it seems more realistic to describe many of us as being owned by our dogs—given the amount of organic chicken and chiropractic appointments we provide for them.

thinking through the difficulty of the exercise, and inadvertently setting him up to fail. Smart trainers learn that their primary job is to control the outcome of a dog's behavior—if he learns that ignoring you leads to an exhilarating chase after a rabbit, how likely is he to listen the next time?

Always consider the level of competing distractions before you call your dog to come when he's still in training. We find it useful to compare come training with levels of mathematical ability: for your dog, coming when there's nothing else going on and you have a piece of chicken in your hand is like adding two and two. Coming away from the fresh scent of deer tracks in the back yard is akin to solving a quadratic equation. Would you expect a seven-year old child to be able to do advanced math? How about expecting a student to skip from simple addition to complicated mathematical formulas without learning algebra? You'd never expect that of your child (we hope), so don't expect it of your dog.

If you're pretty sure your dog-in-training is too distracted to respond at any particular time, simply go *to him* with a treat in hand, show him the treat and lure him to where you want him to go. Give yourself a treat if you do this, (chocolate kisses in your other pocket?) because it seems to be against human nature to walk closer to our dogs instead of standing still and calling in a louder voice. If a treat an inch from his nose isn't enough to get his attention, snap on his leash and gently ease him along to where you need to go. Of course, ideally you'll do all you can to avoid putting him in situations over his head, but even the best of trainers have to go get their dogs on occassion. Additionally, avoid calling your dog for something he's not going to enjoy, like getting a nail trim or going into his crate if he's still full of energy. In that case, simply go to him and snap on his leash, keep a friendly and upbeat attitude, and be sure to avoid linking the word come with something he doesn't like.

TOOLS OF THE TRADE

THE RIGHT TOOL FOR THE JOB People who work with large animals know that you have to have the right equipment to handle them effectively and humanely. Most of us don't think of dogs as large animals, unless, of course, you have a Great Dane or an Irish Wolfhound.

However, even a medium-sized dog can be tremendously powerful—just ask anyone who's been hauled through the neighborhood by a thirty-pound dog.

Small dogs can morph into draft horses as soon as you click on the leash for the same reason that horses can pull wagons. Any four-legged animal can use their entire body, especially their hindquarters, to push into a collar and propel whatever is attached in a forward direction. Horses don't actually pull wagons; they push into the "collar" (which is actually the biggest part of a harness). Because the collar is attached to the wagon, the wagon gets helplessly hauled forward, but the horse is actually pushing against the collar, just like your dog pushes against his own collar. If you feel like you're being hauled helplessly down the street like a wagon, now you know why. Of course, our dogs' collars rest on their throats rather than their chests, but dogs are remarkably resistant to something pushing against the front of their throat, as everyone knows whose walks are accompanied by the sound of a gagging dog who is relentlessly straining to go faster than his pokey old human.

The old-fashioned solutions to this problem involve using a "choke" or "training" collar that tightens as the dog pulls harder, or a "prong" collar with spikes that pressed into the dog's neck. There's no denying that both of these methods can work for some people, but more often they either hurt or scare the dog, or just simply don't work. Choke collars are especially ineffective because dogs are amazingly resistant to increasing levels of pressure around their neck. Prong collars can hurt dogs and/or elicit defensive aggression. However, there are new products on the market that radically improve things for both people and dogs. They are designed to get physics on your side so that you can walk side-by-side with your dog without having to be hauled down the sidewalk like a helpless victim.

Once a dog is trained to walk at your side without pulling we advise using a buckle collar and four to six-foot leash. However, dogs don't come pre-programmed to stroll beside you like your human friends do, so until a dog has some training under his collar you need an effective and humane way of controlling him. Our favorite device at the moment is called a "body harness." Given what we just said about draft horses using harnesses to pull wagons, our recommendation

People who work with large animals know that you have to have the right equipment to handle them effectively and humanely.

might seem counter-intuitive, but these harnesses have the leash attached at the *front* of your dog's chest, not at the top of the back. Thus, your dog can't sink his body forward and push against the chest band. This allows you to steer and control your dog, rather than stimulating him to pull against you. We've found that almost all the dogs in our consultations and training classes respond well to these harnesses, and appear to be perfectly comfortable with them from the moment they are first fitted. There are several brands on the market, including the original, the Sense-sation™ harness by Softouch Concepts and the Easy Walk™ Harness by Premier.

Another good solution for some dogs is the "head collar," which was the first effective and humane solution to walking a dog who was more interested in chasing a chipmunk than walking beside you. Head collars look like the halters that horses wear, and allow you to control your dog's actions by controlling the orientation of his head. When you pull on the leash, the dog's nose and eyes are directed toward you. Dogs tend to think about what they're looking at, so once you have your dog looking at you, you're likely to have his attention as well. Head collars work beautifully for some dogs, and we like them especially for extra-large and extra-exuberant dogs whose owners need as much physics on their side as they can get. However, some dogs don't seem to like them, and spend much of the time trying to paw them off.

Keep in mind that all these devices are management tools, and aren't substitutes for good training. Once trained and matured, many dogs will walk beside you happily and politely on a simple buckle collar and a loose leash. But all dogs are different, and some dogs will always be a little bit more challenging than others. There's no reason not to use a harness or head collar for the rest of your dog's life if that's what works best for both of you. After all, no one apologizes for walking a horse on a halter.

Dogs don't come pre-programmed to stroll beside you like your human friends do.

WEEKLY SUMMARY

What's this? Homework? Well… call it what you will, but training is like a sport, and neither you nor your dog are going to work well together if you don't practice. The good news is that using positive reinforcement means that it's fun for both of you. You don't have to be perfect, and you can scatter your training "sessions" throughout the day. You may not have an extra hour in every day, but even the busiest of us have an extra thirty seconds.

Remember that we've designed this book as a six-week program, so, if you can, commit yourself to jumping in with all paws during this time period, knowing that "training" will soon become part and parcel of your daily life.

Here's a summary of what to focus on this week:

• TREATS Let your dog show you what she's most willing to work for, and take the time to stock up on treats and/or toys that are easily accessible. Many professional trainers prepare training treats once a week, and keep small plastic bags of them in the freezer so that they always have fresh, yummy treats handy when they need them.[7]

• POSITIVE REINFORCEMENT Your job in this phase of training is to set your dog up to win, and to prevent losses. Focus this week on teaching your dog that learning is fun, that listening to you is fun, and that she's really, really glad to be in school. Use the treats that she loves the most, and practice reinforcing her instantly when she does what you ask.

• PRAISE Consciously link up your praise word with something that makes your dog feel good, especially those tasty treats we've talked about. Say "Good!" or "Yes!" and immediately hand or toss your dog a tasty treat. Use the same word consistently (always the hardest part for us humans!) and be sure to only use the word when you're sure your dog is about to be very, very happy.

---

[7] Many professional trainers also regularly wash their jeans with dog treats still in the pockets, but that practice is not recommended.

• THE NAME GAME Several times a day, take your dog into an environment with low-level distractions (both inside and outside) and say his name, just once. As soon as he turns his head toward you, praise and treat. If he ignores you, walk a few feet away from the direction of his focus, and then try again. Work on saying his name only once, and letting him be the one to initiate looking at you once you've said his name. Be especially generous with treats if the distraction turned out to be more difficult than you'd anticipated, and your dog still came through without any prompting. If your dog won't look at you after several attempts, move to a less distracting environment, let him sniff the treats in your hand and then try again as soon as he turns his head away.

• SIT Practice the lure/reward method to teach your dog to sit using both visual and verbal cues. If your dog won't sit down as you lure the treat toward his tail, try moving him so that he's facing out of a corner, and can't back up without hitting a wall. Remember not to say "sit" until you're sure he will sit when lured, then start saying it *before* you move your hand. Once you've had a couple of sessions of successful luring, try moving your hand in an upward sweep toward you, rather than over his head. By the end of the week you could easily have a dog who sits, if not too distracted, every time you signal with your hand.

• COMING WHEN CALLED Be sure to practice all week in areas with few distractions, but vary the time of day and location. Make coming when called into a fun game that your dog loves to play, being sure to use the same cue every time, to keep sessions short, and to not call when your dog is too far away. Remember the value of turning *away* from your dog as you call, and reinforcing with praise the instant he turns toward you. And don't forget to treat, treat, treat when he gets all the way to you!

COMMUNICATION

This week's focus is on communication, both from your perspective and from that of your dog. First, it's worthwhile to look at how dogs communicate to other dogs, without humans muddying the waters.

CHEMICAL COMMUNICATION Chemical signals are the dog's primary means of exploring the world. Some favorite dog smells include rotten fish, fresh cow manure, and bitches in heat. You can use any of these things to get a dog's attention, although we wouldn't recommend it. As luck would have it, you can also send out some interesting chemical signals without carrying a smelly fish or a lusty Pomeranian in your pocket. Liver, chicken or high quality dog treats are great for getting your dog's attention. Food smells are an especially useful way to lure your dog into a desired posture, as you did when teaching sit in the last chapter. We know from psychology experiments that animals learn fastest if they are allowed to initiate an action themselves, rather than being forced (even gently) into it, and luring with food can jumpstart that process. We also know that the sense of smell is tightly linked to the emotional system of mammals—the good smells of food not only get your dog's attention, they act to condition him to feel good when he does what you ask.

VERBAL COMMUNICATION Professional trainers know that it's not so much *what* you say to your dog, it's *how* you say it. Your dog will assume you are displeased with him if you say "Great!" in a low, growly voice. However, he'll think you're happy if you say "I hate you!" with a soft, rolling tone. That's because dogs attend to pitch and other elements of sound more than they do to the actual words. High, squeaky noises are perceived to be excited, friendly or appeasing, while

Professional trainers know that it's not so much what you say to your dog, it's how you say it.

low, growly noises are authoritative or inhibiting. If you belt out "Spot COME!" in a gruff voice your dog will think you are telling him to stay away. If you say "No! No!" in a high, wavering voice your dog probably thinks you're saying "Yes! Yes! Wasn't that fun! Let's do it again!"

The length and form of a verbal cue is also important to your dog's response. Cues that ask your dog to be active should be short, repeated notes like "pup, pup, pup" or handclaps and smooches. On the other hand, inhibiting words or phrases are most effective if they are made up of only one note. If you say them slowly, like "Staaaaay," you can slow or calm your dog. If you say them abruptly, like "WHOA!" you have a better chance of stopping a dog who is already in motion.

VISUAL COMMUNICATION Although the way you talk to your dog is important, keep in mind that dogs primarily use visual signals to communicate with one another. If you learn anything from this book, learn this! While you are talking, your dog is watching every little move that you make. Of course dogs can learn all kinds of word cues, but research and practical experience both show that visual cues overwhelm spoken ones if presented simultaneously. This is probably the most common cause of miscommunication with dogs—you think they are responding to your spoken "sit" when they have actually learned to sit when you rock your body forward or move your hand. We often aren't aware of how our body moves, and so, unknowingly, we change our visual cues from time to time. Inevitably, our dogs become confused and eventually learn to ignore us. However, we can use our dog's attention to movement to our advantage. It just takes some awareness of what we're doing with our bodies when we're working with our dog.

Dogs are so responsive to movement that some visual cues don't even have to be taught. Dogs naturally respond to squatting or bowing down as if it were the "play bow" of a littermate, and come running to play. Alternatively, if you stand tall and move abruptly forward you can often stop a dog in his tracks. Other visual cues do have to be taught, but dogs appear to learn them very fast, especially if they are linked with the lure/reward method. For example, as you moved food toward a dog's tail to lure him into a sit, you were also moving your hand. The hand movement itself becomes a cue to sit, and is actually much easier to teach than a sit to a word cue.

Although the way you talk to your dog is important, keep in mind that dogs primarily use visual signals to communicate with one another.

IT IS ALL ABOUT YOU!

WHO IS TRAINING WHOM? Given what you've read so far, you can see why "dog training" is as much about people as it is about dogs. And why not? Why should you know how to train dogs just because you love them? Should you be able to repair your car because you love cars? Not necessarily; you might love hot showers, but that doesn't mean you could fix a broken pipe. But you could learn. All great dog trainers start out by understanding that dog training is a science, a sport and a bit of an art. It's not rocket science, honest, it just takes a bit of knowledge and practice to get good at it.

With that in mind, this week focus on your own behavior as much as your dog's. A big part of becoming a good dog trainer is learning that *everything* you do means something to your dog. Your actions, no matter how subtle, can either confuse him or help him understand what you want. Because of that, the more you practice moving in specific, precise ways (ones that often don't come naturally), the better behaved your dog will be. Work on establishing clear cues that you use consistently, and on eliminating extraneous sounds and actions from your repertoire. We'll emphasize this aspect of training in each exercise of this chapter, because it's so important. Always keep in mind that much of your dog's behavior happens in response to your behavior. Oh the power!

> *A big part of becoming a good dog trainer is learning that everything you do means something to your dog.*

THIS WEEK'S EXERCISES

TRAINING THE SIT CUE – WITH BOTH YOU AND YOUR DOG AS THE STUDENTS

SORTING OUT THE CUES Dogs are often "disobedient" because they are confused about the cues we use when asking them to do something. For example, asking a dog to sit sounds like child's play, but in actuality it takes practice to do it clearly and consistently. We humans aren't inherently very good at that; we say "sit" one day and "sit down" the next. Additionally, we often signal our dogs without knowing it—we unconsciously lean forward the slightest bit when we say "sit," and our dogs think our forward movement is the cue, not the word we spoke. This difference in focus between human and dogs can lead to lots of confusion, but it can be easily prevented if you pay particular attention to how your own behavior affects your dog's behavior.

For example, last week, you worked on luring your dog to sit by moving a treat up and over his head. After a few successful repetitions, you began to say the word "sit" before you moved your hand. Your dog received two different cues—a spoken word and a movement—each of which means "please sit." This week, your job is to be clear in your own mind about which one you are using, and to help your dog learn to respond to each of them separately.

First of all, ask your dog to sit as you did last week, using both the word sit and the movement of your hand up and back over his head. After repeating this once or twice, notice if you are saying the word "sit" *before* you begin moving your arm. It is important to do so, because visual cues trump verbal ones if they are given simultaneously. If you move your arm at the *same time* that you say sit, your dog will focus on the movement and be less likely to learn to respond to the verbal cue. It's handy to have a dog who sits in response to either a sound or a motion, so begin keeping them separate as you practice this week.

Practice a few times saying "sit" well before you move your hand. After a few successful repetitions, try saying "sit" by itself, without moving your hand or body in any way. Wait a few seconds, perhaps three or four, to give your dog a chance to sit using the word alone. If she does, have a party, giving her exuberant praise and some extra treats for being so clever, and then try it again.

Once your dog has learned to respond to the work "sit" without a visual cue, alternate between using either the word or the motion all by itself.

If, however, she continues to stand still, looking as if she's waiting for you to tell her what to do, help her by using the movement of your arm as a cue. Resist the oh-so-common urge to repeat the word sit—that will teach her to ignore it the first time she hears it, and to wait for you to repeat it to her. Once she's complied, reinforce her with a treat, and go back to a few repetitions of sit with both cues used simultaneously. Try using the verbal cue by itself a few repetitions later, remembering to give her lots of enthusiastic praise and treats if she complies to the sound of your voice by itself. However, don't worry if she won't sit in response to the word alone yet—all dogs learn at different paces, and some are more visual than others. Just keep working at it, concentrate on your own behavior, and train yourself to be conscious about what you say and how you move your arm.

Once she has learned to respond to the word "sit" without a visual cue, alternate between using either the word or the motion all by itself. When working on her visual cue, concentrate on moving your arm in an upward motion toward your body, rather than a movement up and backward over her head. Sometimes ask for a sit with a motion, sometimes just with the word, always being ready to go back to combining them if necessary. Be sure to give her a few extra treats if she responds when she is distracted. Remember that most dogs respond to visual cues better than they do to verbal ones, so be prepared to spend more time working on her response to the word all by itself. Try for two or three short sessions of this scattered through the day, asking for a sit no more than five or six times in a row.

SWAP HANDS This is also a good week to transition from always having a treat in the hand you use to cue your dog. Wait for a time when there are no distractions and your dog is hungry. Ask your dog to sit with a visual cue, but this time hold the treat in your *other* hand—the one that you aren't using to cue your dog. We want your dog to learn that something good will come from doing what you ask, even if she can't smell something wonderful in the hand she's watching. If she doesn't sit when asked, let her smell the treat in your other hand, then ask again. Of course, as soon as she sits, immediately offer her the treat from the hand with the goodies.

One note of caution: we've suggested changing two things from last week—taking the food out of your signal hand and using one cue at a time. Work on these changes separately, working on both simultaneously might be too much for some dogs. It's only the second week of training after all! You be the judge, and only ask your dog to do what you think she is capable of doing. You're actually asking quite a lot of her—so remember how important it is to build on success rather than set up failure. Be sure to vary the location, time of day and duration of each of your sessions, but do be consistent about asking her to sit when there are few or no distractions to muddle things up.

THE NAME GAME

KEEP IT UP! Continue to practice the name game, paying conscious and careful attention to the way you say your dog's name. Do you say it the same way every time, or do you alternate between different words and tones of voice? Listen to everyone in the family, and do what you can to establish one clear and consistent sound that is used to get your dog's attention. (Training all members of the family to be consistent is much harder than training a dog. If you pull it off quickly and smoothly, please write us and tell us how you did it.)

If your dog is responding well when there are no distractions, try gradually increasing the level of distraction from non-existent to mild or moderate. It's helpful to write down a list of distractions and assign them scores based on how much they compete for your dog's attention. For example, your list might look something like this, 0 being easiest and 10 being hardest, assuming you have tasty treats in your hand:

Dog alone with me in kitchen, no one else home 0

Dog alone with me in kitchen, kids playing in next room 2

Outside in backyard, nothing visible going on 5
(think of all the smells!)

Outside in backyard, squirrel chattering by fence 8

Outside in front yard, dog walking by 60 ft away 6

Outside in front yard, your dog has just found
potato chips in the grass 9

Visitors ringing the door bell 10

Playing with another dog . . . . .12 (!)

Of course, every dog is different, and your dog may be more distracted by a squirrel than visitors. That's why you need to be thoughtful about what distracts your dog, and to plan your training accordingly. Great dog trainers are always conscious of how hard an exercise is for each dog as an individual, and patiently work up through increasing levels of distractions. At this stage in training you'd be wise to stick with the easier half of the scale, setting your dog up to win rather than to fail.

Remember to say your dog's name only once, and then let him make his own decision to look at you or not. Your job is to say his name, wait for his head to turn toward you and then immediately praise and treat. This all sounds so very simple, but truth be told, it's hard to keep from repeating the dog's name if he doesn't respond. It takes faith and patience to wait for a dog to turn his head on his own after you've said his name. After he does, most of us wait too long to praise and treat our dogs. We say "Chipper," our dog turns to look at us and for an endless period of two to three seconds, nothing happens. Except something does happen—Chipper learns that there's no reason to turn and look at you, because there's nothing going on in your direction and there are more interesting things happening elsewhere. Practice saying "Good!" the instant his head starts to turn, and notice how much faster your dog progresses.

A little attention to these tips will go a long way toward having a dog who gives you his undivided attention when you ask for it. If you've gotten to the point of always saying your dog's name once and only once and reinforcing him the instant his head turns, please walk into the kitchen and give yourself lots of chocolate! Good human!

Practice saying "Good!" the instant your dog's head starts to turn, and notice how much faster your dog is progressing.

LIE DOWN

This is a wonderful thing to teach your dog, because it can keep your dog out of all kinds of trouble. You might use it when Goldie gets a bit too excited during a play session, or combine it with your stay cue when you need a little peace and quiet during dinner. Dogs who are lying down aren't barking hysterically out the window, aren't running toward the road, and aren't chasing the neighbor's children in the back yard. The benefit of having a dog who happily lies down when asked is well worth the time it takes to create a solid foundation. Lying down on cue takes a bit longer to teach than sitting on cue, but if you use the lure/reward method you can make rapid progress.

Begin by putting a tasty treat in your hand, and asking your dog to sit. Move the treat to within an inch of your dog's nose, and then slowly move the treat straight down toward the ground. Most dogs will follow the treat with their nose, and their bodies will follow their nose down to the ground. You might have to hold the treat on the ground for a few seconds before your dog lies all the way down, but be patient. Sometimes it helps to tap the ground with your hand to attract her attention. Most importantly, be sure to move the treat straight down below your dog's nose. If you move your hand even slightly forward, your dog will get up to get the treat, and you'll have to start all over again. Don't worry when that happens—if Goldie gets up out of the sit, just ask for it again, and then lure her nose down toward the ground, being careful to move your hand slowly so that your dog doesn't lose the scent of the treat.

Notice at this point we haven't suggested saying "lie down" or "down." Things will go more smoothly if you don't say anything until after you're sure your dog is lying down to the lure. Once you can count on your dog to lie down as you move the treat toward the ground, say "down" *before* you begin the movement. Eventually, your dog will respond to both a hand movement and the word cue by itself, but for now, do all you can to help her lie down by luring her nose toward the ground.

TROUBLESHOOTING There are a few dogs who haven't read this part of the chapter, and in spite of your best efforts, never quite make it down to the ground. If that's happening to you, there are a variety of things you can try to help your dog lie down when you ask. If she keeps backing up instead of lying down, you can try having her sit with her back to a corner, so that she can't back up. If the problem isn't backing up, but your dog seems stuck on the sit and just can't make it all the way down, you can try one of two things. While continuing to lure, try placing your hand on her back, just an inch behind her shoulder blades (fingers on one side, thumb on the other) and gently, gently push slightly sideways and downward. Be ready to praise and treat the instant she lies down.

You can also try luring her under a horizontal bar such that she has to lie down and crawl to get under it. Set it up so there's no way for her to go around it (perhaps in your hallway) and low enough that she has to lie down to crawl under it. Present an extra tasty treat close to the ground on the other side of the bar, and use it to lure her underneath. The instant that she lies down in order to crawl, say "Good!" and give her the treat. You can even use an extended leg as a bar if your dog is

The benefit of having a dog who happily lies down when asked is well worth the time it takes to create a solid foundation.

small enough—a procedure not recommended if you have a Newfoundland. Once your dog reliably lies down to crawl, you can raise the bar and eventually eliminate it entirely.

A few last comments about dogs who just don't want to lie down when asked: Some dogs, especially thin-skinned, slender ones, don't like lying down on a cold, hard surface. If you think this might describe your dog, try asking her to lie down on a rug or towel, and see if that makes a difference. Also, dogs don't like to lie down if they're a bit nervous, anymore than we do. Do you want to lie down when you are feeling insecure and nervous in a strange place? If this might explain your dog's behavior, try working on this at home when your dog is calm and relaxed. If you're still having trouble at home, try saying "lie down" every time your dog chooses to lie down herself. Then praise and treat, just as if you'd ask for it yourself. After awhile, you can say "lie down" when you *think* your dog is about to, and eventually you'll be able to use it to get your dog to settle to the floor.

Most dogs, bless them, are happy to lie down when lured with a treat, so most people can concentrate this week on luring their dog into a down. Once that's working, be sure to say the cue *before* you move your hand. Remember that dogs don't need to learn to lie down, any more than they need to learn to sit. What you're teaching is lying down "on cue," which means you should be working as hard as your dog—ensuring that your cues are consistent (both visual and verbal), your timing is good (praise the instant she lies down and deliver a treat right away) and that you're working on this in areas with little or no distraction.

FOUR ON THE FLOOR

You don't need us to tell you why teaching your dog not to jump up is an important part of family dog training. You may not mind your dog jumping up when you're outside in your gardening clothes, but you probably aren't fond of muddy paws on your chest when you're on your way to an important meeting. The dog-loving friends in your life may not mind when your ninety-pound Labrador slaps his front paws on their shoulders, but the UPS man might. It can take time and patience to teach a dog to keep his paws on the ground, but it's worth the effort. Remember that jumping up isn't rude in dog society—polite dogs greet familiar dogs by sniffing or licking one another's muzzles. It's not their fault you put your own muzzle so high up in the air that they have to leap up toward it! I suspect that, from their perspective, we're the ones who are being rude.

GETTING STARTED Ask a friend or family member to help you out and start with some tasty treats ready in your hand. You can work on this anywhere that your dog might jump up, but doorways are an especially good place to start. Ask your helpers to approach your dog (family members can go out of the house and come in the front door), and as soon as they get within a few feet of your pup, have them ask your dog to sit. If he sits as asked, you should immediately praise and give him a treat. In other words, the *visitor* asks for the sit, but *you* give your dog the treat. The visitor should ask for the sit because it's easier for a dog to respond to the person facing them. If *you* ask for the sit, you're asking him to sit facing away from you, and that's harder for dogs at this stage of training. However, it's still best at this stage if you are the one to provide the treat.

Repeat this exercise four or five times, ending before your dog gets bored with the game, but when he's responding well. However, it's always good to have a back up plan if things don't go as intended. If your dog doesn't sit at all, even when asked clearly, don't worry. Go ahead and ask him to sit yourself, moving around so that you are facing him before asking. Try that a few times and then have the visitor ask again. If your dog keeps jumping up—and let's face it, some of them do—don't say anything, but instruct the visitor to abruptly turn and walk away. That way the dog learns that the object of his excitement goes away if he jumps up. Wait four or five seconds, then have the visitor approach again. Keep it up until your dog sits as asked, and then give him several pieces of food to be sure he's glad he finally got a hold of himself! Be careful, though, to keep your voice quiet and calm. You might even skip praise altogether with dogs who get extra excited around company; sometimes just the sound of your voice can hype them up again. If that describes your dog, let the food do the talking. If jumping up on visitors is a big problem, always work at a doorway so that you can have the person turn and shut the door behind them if the dog jumps up rather than sitting.

Remember that jumping up isn't rude in dog society – polite dogs greet familiar dogs by sniffing or licking each other's muzzles.

ME TOO You can teach your dog to keep his paws on the ground when he greets you by using the same methods you are using with visitors. Think through all the situations in which your dog might jump on you, and be mentally prepared to ask him to sit before he does. That means thinking ahead: get in the habit of pausing before you open the door to the house when you get home from work, or when you open the door to his crate. Remind yourself to ask for a sit as soon as your dog is within six feet of you (yes, that far away!), using an exaggerated upward sweep of your arm to help him when he's likely to be a bit excited. Of course, you'll have thought ahead and will have a treat already out and in your hand. (It works well to have a treat basket hanging right outside the door to your house.) Remember that you'll need to exercise your own emotional control when you enter the house—though that can be hard to do when you're thrilled to see your dog! Even so, do your best to keep your voice quiet and your body movements calm, or you'll end up exciting your dog into jumping up, in spite of his best efforts to be polite.

You can even set up training sessions in which you go in and out of your house, using all the doors anyone might ever enter, and ask for a sit each time you enter the house. Use the same rules you did before, and begin by asking for a sit either verbally or with a hand motion. If your dog sits on his own without a cue from you, be ready with a "jackpot" of ten treats in a row. This week, be sure to work on this as often as you can when he's relatively relaxed. Of course, that's when he's least likely to jump up, but that's when you want to start—when he has the best chance of doing it right, so that you can reinforce him.

If Fido is just too darned excited to sit for you, even if you asked ever-so-clearly, simply turn away so that all he can see is your back. This deters most dogs, but not all of them. If your dog is one of the pushy and creative ones, and responds to your turning away by jumping up on your backside, work on this at a doorway. If you turn away and he counters by climbing your derriere as if it was a mountain peak, just walk outside and shut the door behind you. Don't talk to him, don't ask for sit a second time, don't pass go and don't collect $200. The trick, as it so often is, is in the timing. Try to teach your dog that he'll lose your attention the instant that he jumps up, but that he'll get treats and/or quiet praise if he sits down. Don't expect a jumper to sit for a long period of time—that's asking too much. Ask for the sit, give him a treat as soon as you get it, and then immediately move away and direct him to a toy or into the backyard. Your job is to get him out of "greeting mode" and focused onto something beside licking your muzzle.

HANDS OFF Avoid doing what seems to come naturally, which is pushing dogs away with your hands. Dogs respond to this as if you were playing, and leap back with even more enthusiasm. It's also very common for people to say "down" when dogs jump up on them. But think about it: down isn't the problem, it's jumping up in the first place! All dogs are going to go down eventually! Besides, aren't you teaching your dog to lie down to "down?" Using the word to mean two different things—lie down and don't jump up—is just another way to confuse your dog.

Avoid doing what seems to come naturally, which is pushing dogs away with your hands.

AN OUNCE OF PREVENTION Sometimes circumstances don't lend themselves to relaxed and effective training sessions. There's nothing wrong with anticipating a situation that is over your dog's head, and putting him in another room or behind a gate while you open the door to visitors. A harassed UPS carrier or your dog-hating Uncle Nick isn't the best person to help you out, and trying to train an overly exuberant dog in those circumstances is just going to add to your stress level. The more stressed you are about your dog not jumping up the more likely he is to do it, so do what most dog professionals do, and take the pressure off.

It's relatively easy to teach a dog to run to another room when the bell rings, as long as you begin practicing before actual visitors arrive. Simply go to the front door when all is quiet, knock or ring the bell yourself, and then dash into the designated room with your dog, calling and clapping as if it was the best game in town. Give your dog a hollow toy stuffed with food and shut the door. Wait just a few seconds, then enter the room and take the toy away and let your dog out. If you time this right, he'll be thinking "wait, don't let me out. I wasn't done yet!" Repeat this two or three times, establishing the pattern: *doorbell rings—dog runs to other room and is glad he did—gets to eat great snacks until mom or dad comes back and takes them away.*

In the second or third session, go back to the front door while your dog is closed inside another room, happily slurping on peanut butter or cheese, and talk as though you are greeting visitors. Next, try having real visitors enter the house for a few minutes. Once the visitor has entered, let your dog out, and practice the "no jump" training as described above. If your visitor isn't the type to want to help you with your dog, either let your dog stay in the other room chewing on his toy, or bring him out on a leash.

This exercise can pay off for years to come. Aimee and I can't count how many times it's been helpful to run our pack of dogs into another room and sign for a package in peace. You might want to work on this even if your dog doesn't jump up, using a silly cue that makes everybody laugh like "get out of town."

SOMEBODY HELP ME! I CAN'T CONTROL MYSELF! Although many dogs learn to control their impulses and keep their paws on the ground in relatively little time, some dogs simply don't have enough emotional control to stop themselves from leaping up when they're excited. Even these dogs can eventually learn to calm down, but meanwhile we've found it useful to give them a chew toy stuffed with food on which to focus while you chat with your guests. Try having the visitor take the toy and show it to your dog, and then ask him to sit. The instant the dog sits, *before* he pops up again like a piece of bread out of an exuberant toaster, have your guest hand him the toy. (You should be ready with treats and praise in case the visitor's timing is off.) Once they have the toy, most dogs can't resist settling down to lick out the food, and by the time they're done your visitors are settled on the couch, the greeting ceremony is long over and Fido is less likely to practice the high jump.[8]

It's relatively easy to teach a dog to run to another room when the bell rings, as long as you begin practicing before actual visitors arrive.

COME

THE JOY OF COMING WHEN CALLED This is a great time to listen to yourself, and the rest of your family, when you call your dog to come. Does the cue vary from "come!" to "Maggie, come here!"? A great family exercise is to tape everyone calling the dog to come, and then sit down together and listen to what is said. Does everyone use the same word? Most important, does everyone say it the same way? Dogs are listening to

---

[8] Try stuffing food into a hollow toy and then putting it in the freezer. It takes dogs longer to lick out frozen snacks, and can keep them busy for a longer period of time.

the tone as much as they are to the syllables, so practice saying the same thing, the same way, every time you call your dog to come.

Also, start working this week on scattering come games throughout the day, calling your dog to come out of the blue. Of course, you still want to be careful not to call your dog away from a major distraction, so work on automatically evaluating the level of competing distractions. If you are 80% sure your dog will come when called, then go ahead and call. Don't do it without a treat (have it in your hand *before* you call!) and be ready to praise the instant you get a response and to have a party when he catches up to you. At this point, be sure to call come when you're no more than six or ten feet away.[9] If you are farther away your dog will be less likely to come, and at this stage it's important to ensure success.

Avoid having your dog associate coming when called with something he doesn't like.

Your focus this week is on calling him to come only one or two times in a row, but doing it in every room, at any time during the day. You want him to learn to come any time you call, no matter where he is and what he is doing. You also want to avoid having him associate your cue with something he doesn't like, so at this point, just go get him if you have to trim his nails or end a play session in the backyard. Try adding another reinforcement this week: as usual, praise him just as soon as his head turns toward you, but then run away from him as soon as he starts to move toward you. Most dogs will think you've initiated a chase game, and there's little a dog loves more than getting to run after you. By making yourself "it," you're adding yet another reason why it's fun to come when called. Stop running before he gets up to you, because we don't want him to get overly excited and start nipping at your trousers. Turn toward him as he completes his last few strides, and then give him that wonderful treat you've gotten out before you called. Aim for a total of 15 or 20 repetitions a day, remembering that it only takes a few seconds each time you call.

WHAT DO I DO IF HE DOESN'T COME WHEN I CALL? Good question, because we guarantee it's going to happen. Perfect little puppies turn into willful adolescents who stop thinking that you're the center of the universe, and older dogs can be so engrossed in the smells on the ground that they act as though they can't hear you (of course they

---

[9] Some dogs will be responsive at a greater distance, but be conservative at this point in training, and guard against calling when your dog is too far away to pay attention to you.

can hear a can opener a half a mile away, but you calling come from ten feet?—nah…). First, here's what NOT to do: do not keep calling come, repeating the word (and its variants) over and over again. If your dog doesn't come to the first cue, give him the benefit of the doubt and say his name clearly and firmly, then call "come!" again in a cheerful and upbeat voice. Don't repeat his name or the cue after that. If your words have had no effect, simply walk to him, show him the treat in your hand (make sure it's a good one, even if you have to run into the kitchen to get it) and see if you can lure him away from what's distracting him. Give him the treat when he's moved in the right direction for a couple of feet, and another treat for coming all the way to where you *first* called him. If the best of treats aren't competitive with whatever's distracting him—what doggy treat could possibly compete with a dead fish?—quietly snap on his leash or gently take him by the collar, and give him something wonderful when you've arrived at your destination. Mentally make a note to go back one step in his training for that particular distraction, and work on it within the next couple of days.

GOOD DOG (NO MATTER WHAT!) At all costs, avoid correcting your dog if he ignores you at first but eventually comes on his own. Yelling at your dog when he finally does come, frustrated though you might be, will destroy your chance of teaching an effective recall. All you'll be doing is teaching your dog that moving toward you is dangerous and to be avoided, which pretty much describes the opposite of what you want. Aimee and I are the first to admit that sometimes our dogs make us crazy, and that staying calm and patient while being ignored is not the easiest advice to follow. Here's an approach we've found useful when our feelings of love for our dogs were temporarily quelched by our desire to wring their adorable little necks. If your little darling completely ignores you, but then finally ambles over just about the time you've decided to give her away, say, in the sweetest, happiest voice imaginable, "Ginger! So good to see you! Perhaps I should mention that, at the moment, I hate every single hair on your body." (Remember, you're cooing out the words as if reciting a romantic poem.) "If you ever do that again I'll sell you to first buyer in an auction." Feel free to make up your own version. This allows you to vent your frustrations and to reinforce your dog for coming at the same time. Your dog will be glad she came if you sound truly happy, and you can

At all costs, avoid correcting your dog if he ignores you at first but eventually comes on his own.

use language to express your frustration, and to remind yourself that, at least this time, you really are smarter than your dog.

HOW LONG WILL THIS TAKE? That depends on how you define a dog who "comes when called." If you want a dog who turns on a dime and runs like Lassie to your side after flushing a fox, then the answer should be given in units of months or years. (And to be honest, for some dogs, never . . .). However, if you want a dog who comes *almost* all of the time you call, even if highly distracted, you'll want to work very hard on this for at least three to six months, and then continue the training with less intensity until the dog is at least three years old. What? Three years old? Well, yes, dogs aren't really grown up until they're three, and just like humans, they have to grow up to have the kind of impulse control and emotional maturity it takes to be reliable. However, before you toss this book in the trash, take heart, because after three to six months of work, you can realistically have a dog who is coming reliably through low and moderate levels of distractions. That means that after three to six months of training, your dog will come when called out of the backyard, no matter what, and for some dogs, even at the dog park when distracted by other dogs.

Always be aware of your dog's ability to control his impulses and his ability to make mature decisions.

The trick is to have a working knowledge of your dog's ability to control his impulses and his ability to make mature decisions. Know what most distracts him, and therefore when you're better off walking (not running) toward him and fetching him yourself rather than calling him to come. Keep in mind that every dog is different—you might have your own Lassie who always comes when called, but even top trainers can have a dog who can never be trusted off-leash in some circumstances—so know your dog and know the level of distraction he is capable of ignoring.

STAY

Staying when told is another wonderful skill to teach your dog. It allows you to settle your dog down when you'd like a few quiet moments in the evening, or to keep her out of trouble so you can check out the strange noise in the backyard.[10] Staying in place teaches your dog patience and impulse control, and can prevent one of the

---

[10] This is not just a theory: I once untangled a deer caught in a fence while my dogs were on a down/stay. I don't want to think about what would have happened if they hadn't listened to me.

most common behavioral problems we see in our office: an inability to cope with frustration, or the doggy equivalent of road rage. Dogs who learn to stay when asked can be much more fun to live with, and are probably happier themselves after learning how to control themselves and their own emotions.

There are three components to a great stay: *Duration*, or the amount of time you expect your dog to stay until released, *Distraction*, which is the level of outside activity that is tempting your dog to get up, and *Distance*, which refers to the distance between you and your dog. Think of them as the three "D's," and try to work on only one of them at a time.

Start first with all three factors at the lowest possible level of intensity. That means you are in an area with no distractions and you're only about one to two feet away from your dog (but not looming over her). Put a treat in your non-dominant hand, and then ask your dog to sit. As soon as she does, say "stay" in a low, quiet voice and move the palm of your hand toward your dog as if you were trying to stop traffic. Stand still yourself, looking directly at your dog for the briefest of moments, and then rock forward and give your dog a treat from your left hand (if right-handed). Be sure to move the treat all the way to her; don't dangle it a few inches in front of her nose so that she has to get up to get it. Rather, with an underhanded motion, swing the treat hand all the way underneath her muzzle and give her the treat while she's still sitting.

After you've given her the treat and she's gulped it down, release her with a calm and quiet "okay" or "free." As you say the release word, rock your body back a few inches and let her do whatever she wants. Don't praise her or try to pet her—you want the fun part to be staying in place, not getting up. (Word to the wise: eliminating praise and petting after releasing a dog from stay seems to be hard for people to do, so focus on staying quiet when you release her. It'll pay off, honest.)

Repeat this exercise about four to six times, asking for one to two second stays that are so short as to be almost silly. She'll learn more quickly (as will you!) if you have several brief stay sessions throughout the day. Don't hesitate to throw in a single sit/stay request here and there, at a

Dogs who learn to stay when asked can be much more fun to live with, and are probably happier themselves after learning how to control their own emotions.

Stay training is a great time to practice giving clear and consistent cues with both your voice and your body.

time when your dog might least expect it. Be sure the distraction level is still extremely low, and that she knows you have treats in your hand. Then ask for what's best described as a "micro-stay." Don't be seduced into asking for longer and longer stays this week. This is one of the exercises in which creating a solid foundation by going slowly at the beginning will pay off in spades in just a few weeks. So patience, patience, and more patience—after all, that is what training is trying to develop in your dog, right?

Stay training is another great time to practice giving clear and consistent cues with both your voice and your body. Concentrate on saying "stay" with a low, relatively quiet voice. Your dog is more likely to stay in place if your voice is flat or drops in pitch. If you do the opposite, and say "stay" as if it was a question (which is common), you're more likely to stimulate your dog to get up. Think also about your visual cues: are you using a clear arm and hand movement that is different from your sit cue? Are all the members of your family using the same cues? (If so, give them lots of reinforcement!) Remember that your dog has no idea about the expected outcome of this exercise, and the only way she can figure it out is if you are consistent. Be sure that you are using an equally clear and consistent release word, like "okay" or "free." Try not to confuse your dog by using the same words to both praise and release her. Many people release their dog to the word "good," but if you reserve "good" to mean "I like what you're doing" and "okay" to mean you can get up now," your dog will thank you for it with better behavior.

WEEKLY SUMMARY

Here's the summary of exercises for this week:

• SIT This week put your treats in your other hand, teaching your dog that there's a payoff for sitting on cue even if she can't smell food right in front of her face. Focus your attention on the clarity of each of your cues, working on giving both the visual and the verbal cue clearly and consistently. Practice saying "sit" before you move your arm, and after a few successful repetitions of both, try saying the word alone, without moving your arm. Your goal this week is to have your dog sit reliably in response to either cue, as long as there are no distractions and she is aware you have food somewhere near by.

• NAME GAME Continue practicing the name game, upping the level of distraction from the week before. Be thoughtful about the level of distraction with which you're competing—consider writing a list of increasing levels of distraction so it's clear in your mind. Don't ask your dog to attend to you if the distraction is over level 4 or 5 out of 10. Remember to say your dog's name only once, and wait for him to initiate the action.

• LIE DOWN With a tasty treat in your hand, ask your dog to sit. Squat down beside your dog, and move the treat to within an inch of her nose. Slowly move the treat straight down (not forward), and be ready to praise and pop the treat into her mouth the instant she lies down. Don't use the verbal cue until you've established that she'll lie down in response to the lure. Three or four repetitions of this are enough at one time, but initiate two or three separate sessions throughout the day.

• FOUR ON THE FLOOR Have visitors ask your dog to sit every time they approach your dog. Be sure your dog knows that you have treats in your hand, and be sure that she's not in the midst of a swirl of other, exuberant dogs. The instant she sits, praise and give her a treat. If she anticipates your cue and sits without you asking her to, give her several treats in a row and act like she just won the lottery! Go out of your way to set up training sessions: go in and out of the front door yourself, ask visitors over, and have the entire family participate.

• COMING WHEN CALLED Keep working on making coming when called a fun thing for your dog to do. Scatter "come games" throughout the day, and ask your dog to come to you at different times of the day, from different areas of your home. Try adding in chase games as one of your reinforcements (but don't let them turn into "chase and nip" games!). Resist the urge to repeat saying "come" if your dog doesn't respond, but instead go to your dog and show him the tasty treat in your hand. Then call again from much closer and reinforce him for getting it right, even if it did take a bit of extra effort on your part. Remember to praise the instant he turns toward you, and treat when he gets to you (don't forget to avoid those annoying head pats that most dogs don't like!)

• STAY Ask your dog to sit, and then say "stay" in a low, quiet voice as you briefly hold your hand out, palm facing forward, like a traffic cop. Using an underhanded motion of your other hand, pop a treat in your dog's mouth while he's sitting still, and then rock back a few inches and release him with a clear verbal cue like "okay" or "free." Remember the three "D's" are distance, distraction and duration. This week keep them all at the lowest level of difficulty that you can.

3

UH OH!

WHAT TO DO WHEN YOUR DOG MISBEHAVES It's inevitable that, every once in a while, your dog is going to act more like Dennis the Menace than he is like Lassie. Even the best dog in the world has to learn not to chew on the table leg or to nip at your heels. It's one thing to teach your dog useful behaviors like sit, down and stay, but what should you do when your dog is doing something you *don't* want him to do? Dogs never seem to run out of ways to get into trouble, whether it's barking like a maniac out the window, chewing on your slippers, or chasing the family cat. Life is a lot more pleasant if you know how to respond swiftly and effectively when Duke is doing something he shouldn't.

WHAT NOT TO DO It's worth taking a moment to discuss what not to do, because many of our typical responses aren't very helpful. For example, it seems to be oh-so-human to respond to misbehavior by saying something to our dog that is meaningful to us, but not to her. How many of us have said "Be quiet!" to a barking dog, and never stopped to think that the words are just meaningless noise to anyone other than English speakers? The tendency to yell pointlessly at our dogs sounds foolish when you read about it, but it's a common response when an animal is doing something we don't like. We make things worse by repeating the words at a louder and louder volume, as if yelling will clarify what we are trying to communicate. That's true no matter what kind of animal we're talking to—recently I watched two men try to disentangle a "cattle jam" by yelling "Turn around, TURN AROUND!" to a frightened cow. Granted, you could teach a cow to turn around on cue, but it was doubtful that this particular cow had been the beneficiary of any such training. Remember this story when you are tempted to yell at your dog, and work on getting into the habit of only using words that mean something to her.

Last, but not least, don't take the advice about "getting dominance over your dog" as a solution to misbehavior. Dogs aren't barking out the window or chasing squirrels because they don't respect you as the "alpha pack leader." They're barking, chasing and chewing because that's what dogs do, and because they haven't yet had a chance to learn behavior that we consider polite.[11] Our primary job is to teach our dogs what we do want them to do, rather than scold them for what we *don't*.

WHAT TO DO The first question to ask yourself when your dog is misbehaving is what do you want your dog to be doing instead? You can say "no" until you're blue in the face, but that won't tell your dog what you want him to be doing. After all, there are a thousand things your dog could be doing wrong, and if you say "no" to one, there are still 999 options left. However, there are only a few things that you would like your dog to be doing—your job is to teach him what they are, even when he has other ideas.

Let's take barking out the window as an example. Imagine you've just settled down to eat your dinner, and your dog sees a couple with a stroller walking past your house. Your dog leaps up and launches into vigorous barking and scratching at the window. If you sit at the table and yell "no," you aren't telling your dog anything about what he should be doing instead. Even worse, you are probably adding fuel to the fire by making bark-like noises yourself—what is your dog to think but that you've joined the festivities and that he was right to bark in the first place?

However, what if you quietly grab a treat from your plate (hey, sometimes you have to be creative), go to your dog and distract him with the treat an inch from his nose? Now you've ensured that you've gotten his attention and distracted him away from the source of his barking. If you lure him away from the window and ask him to sit and lie down, you've just shown him what you *do* want him to do. By *interrupting* the problem behavior and then *redirecting* him to something appropriate, you've turned a problem situation into a "teachable moment." You can make

> Our primary job is to teach our dogs what we do want them to do, rather than scold them for what we don't.

11 We'll talk in more depth in the next chapter about misunderstandings related to "dominance," and the importance of teaching dogs to be patient and polite.

a mental note that barking out the window could be an issue that needs your attention, and that you need to proactively teach him a different response when he sees people walking by. You can do that by using your trusty treats or toys to reinforce him every time he turns away from the window after seeing something outside, helping him when necessary by luring him away or clapping your hands to get his attention. Eventually he'll do it all by himself, having learned it's fun to turn away from the window when he sees someone outside.

What if you walk into the room and spot your dog munching away on the remote control? This is another situation in which you want to interrupt the behavior and redirect your dog to something appropriate—like the expensive chew toy you just bought him at the pet store. This is also a time when it's useful to teach your dog a cue that means "nope, please don't do that."

"NO" IS JUST A NOISE There's something seductive about the word "no," but until you teach your dog what it means, no is just noise. It's common for people to say "NO!" to their dog and expect him to under-stand what it means, even when they'd never expect the equivalent with "sit" or "down." The word no is often yelled at full volume, and sometimes it does indeed stop the misbehavior. Yelling can scare many dogs into stopping what they were doing, but do you really want a dog who is scared of you? Besides, it's no fun to be yelling all the time, so it's worth taking the time to teach your dog a cue that means "I'm sorry, but what you're about to do is not allowed here"—without hav-ing to belt it out at the top of your lungs.

First, decide as a family what word or sound you are going to use, and do your best to be consistent when you use it. The word "no" is out of favor with many trainers, probably because it is so often abused, but it's a fine choice if that's what comes naturally. Other common cues are "wrong," "uh uh," and "hey!" Try to be as consistent with this cue as you are with all the others, and work on saying it in a quiet but low-pitched voice.

Armed with your handy treats, set your dog up to do something inappropriate, like chew on your shoes. Select an item that will be of some interest, but that's only mildly attractive to your dog. No fair putting down a bowl of chicken! Set the article on the ground, and say "no" (or its equivalent) as your dog stretches his head toward it. Use a low, quiet voice, but try to have the sound come out of your mouth as fast as it can. You want to startle your dog with a surprising sound, not bowl him over with a loud noise, so keep the volume moderate. If your dog stops moving toward the item in response to your voice, instantly praise and give him a treat. If he doesn't, move the treat to his nose and lure him away from the item. Praise as his head turns, and give him a treat. Then back up one step, and give him a chance to sniff the article again. Say "no," as he moves toward it, doing all you can to say it *before* he makes contact with the item. Respond as before, praising and treating if he stops himself, helping him do the right thing by luring him away if he doesn't.

REMOTE CORRECTIONS Sometimes your dog will start doing something that you have to stop right away, even when he's on the other side of the room. Perhaps he's about to chew on a valuable plant, or he's lunging for the Thanksgiving turkey that fell off the counter. If you're too far away to intervene yourself, and you know saying "no" won't be adequate at his level of training, your best bet is to say "no" and immediately throw something that will land beside him to startle him. Your goal is to startle and redirect him, not frighten or hurt him, so throw something like a paperback book or a magazine that can't hurt him if you miss, and isn't so noisy it will scare him. Every dog is different—some sound sensitive dogs will stop if an issue of Reader's Digest lands lightly at their feet, while others might only respond to a New York City telephone book dropped as if from a skyscraper. Let your dog's responses be your guide, remembering that your goal is to interrupt the behavior and reinforce him for stopping what he was about to do when you said "no."

Your dog, bless his furry little heart, will give you lots of opportunities to practice all of these techniques, whether he's chewing on the table leg, squatting to urinate on the rug, or getting ready to chase the cat up the stairs. The key to making this work is to say the cue as fast as you can, and then be ready—always, always ready!—to make him happy he listened to you. It helps to match the reinforcement with what he was about to do. If he was about to chase the cat, reinforce him by letting him chase you or a ball. If he wanted to chew on your new shoes, give him an appropriate chew toy.

BE PROACTIVE Here's one last comment about preventing dogs from getting themselves (and us) into trouble. We touched on it earlier, but it bears repeating because it's so important. Good dogs are dogs who got into good habits early in life, and who were prevented from learning bad habits as much as possible. Of course, habits can be changed, but we all know it's not as easy as starting from scratch. You'll be happiest with your dog if you are proactive about teaching good habits and preventing problematic ones. This advice sounds so simplistic it almost seems unnecessary, but it takes thought and attention on our part to be one step ahead of our dogs. If your pup starts to bark out the front window every time he sees someone walk by, teach him a different response right away. If you have a dog nicknamed "the mouth with paws," don't wait for him to grab your Italian shoes out of the closet. Prevent problems by being obsessive about keeping your personal items off the floor and shutting doors.

CRATE TRAINING Crates and exercise pens are a wonderful way to keep your dog out of trouble in the short run and prevent bad habits in the long run. Most dogs readily learn that their crate or pen is like a comfy bedroom, but you need to start by following a few simple steps.

~ Don't force your dog into the crate—toss yummy treats inside and let him go in and out freely to get them.

~ Once he'll go in and out of the crate, toss in a few treats, close the door to the crate for a few seconds, and then let him out. Repeat this five or six times, as if it was a fun game you were playing. Try for several sessions of this an hour or two apart.

~ Later in the day, when your dog is getting sleepy, put him in the crate with a chew bone, and shut the door. If he's hungry and/or sleepy, he'll probably chew on the bone for a while, and then drift off to sleep.

~ If you have to crate him when he's full of energy, give him an extra tasty chew bone or stuffed toy, so that he's occupied and happy to be confined.

~ Whenever possible, let him out of the crate before he starts to whine or cry. If he does get fussy, do your best to wait for a time in which he's relatively quiet, and then let him out. (See the book *Puppy Primer* for a more lengthy description of crate training.)

CHAPTER 3

The key to making this work is to get your cue out as fast as you can, and then be ready – always, always ready! – to make him happy he listened to you.

Some dogs become comfortable in a crate within a day or two of training, while others take a bit longer. But all dogs need to start out the same way—learning that the crate is their comfy, private bedroom. It's not true that "dogs are den animals," so they need to be conditioned to be comfortable in a crate.[12] However, once they've learned how cozy crates can be, most dogs learn to love them—all my dogs love to cuddle up in a crate if they have a chance.

IN SUMMARY Do all you can to prevent your dog from developing bad habits and learn to interrupt and redirect him when he's about to get into trouble. If necessary (and it will be), recite daily "this too shall pass," "this too shall pass." It takes a while for good habits to form, but the work is worth years of relaxation and peace. Speaking of good habits, the next section introduces one of the best habits of all to teach your dog—the habit of paying attention.

THIS WEEK'S EXERCISES

PLEASE PAY ATTENTION

"He just won't listen to me!" That's the most common complaint voiced by dog owners, and it represents the flip side of what most of us want from our dogs: their attention. But look at what we're competing against—our dogs are surrounded by a smorgasbord of scents, by interesting movements, and by sounds that need to be investigated. This is particularly problematic when they're outside, and even worse if they're around the ultimate distraction—other dogs (as in dog training classes!).

All this competition from the environment means that smart owners go out of their way to teach their dogs to pay attention to them.

PAYING ATTENTION All this competition from the environment means that we need to go out of our way to teach our dogs to pay attention to us. This is where something called *free shaping* comes in handy, and it's probably the easiest training you'll ever do.[13] All you need to do is put your dog on a leash, go to an area of mild to moderate level distractions and give your dog a tiny, tasty treat every time he

[12] Dogs aren't wolves, and besides, wolves only go into dens when they are giving birth and raising baby wolves.

[13] Free shaping means that you wait for your dog to initiate a behavior and then reinforce it, rather than luring or prompting him to do what you want.

happens to look in your direction. (Be sure to have the treats easily accessible, but don't show them to your dog before you start.) Avoid calling his name or trying to get him to look at you, just wait for the brief moment in which his head turns toward you, praise, and immediately pop a treat in his mouth. Your only job is to keep at least part of your attention on your dog, so that you notice it every time he looks at you. (This can be harder than it sounds, since our species is as easily distracted as are dogs!)

Notice that this exercise differs from the name game, in that this time you aren't asking your dog to do anything. You're allowing him to do whatever he wants, and letting him learn that something good will happen if he chooses to look at you. He'll learn that it pays to check in with "tall two-leg" every once in a while, even when there are other interesting things going on. That's why this exercise is the exception to our relentless advice about doing the first weeks of training in areas with no distractions. In this case, you want your dog to be a bit distracted by something else, although not so much so that there's no chance he'll turn and look toward you.

If you try this and find he hasn't looked in your direction after a minute or two, remain silent, but move a few feet away—often your movement is enough to get your dog's attention. Be ready for the millisecond that he glances at you, even momentarily, praise him and pop a treat in his mouth. Dogs catch on fast after they've gotten the first few treats, and usually start looking at you with increasing frequency. Each time this happens, give your dog a treat. Try this a couple of times a day, varying the length of the session depending upon what else is on your agenda. There's nothing wrong with stopping after just one "look," although early sessions would be most helpful if your dog looks at you somewhere between three to six times. Some dogs will eventually end up staring at you and only you. If that happens, just end the session, and go back inside or continue on your walk.

Don't practice this at home when you're hanging out together in the den, or anywhere in the house when there are no other significant distractions. Take it from a Border Collie owner, you don't want a dog who stands staring at you for hours while you're trying to watch television. But if you play this game when you and your dog are in distracting environments,

Be ready the millisecond that he glances at you, even momentarily, and pop a treat in his mouth.

you'll have a dog who's learned that it always pays to check in with you. It's especially useful in the first weeks of a training class, when out on walks, or in a distracting environment like the lobby of a vet clinic.

Don't worry about having to do this for the rest of your dog's life. You can start decreasing the number of times you give him a treat once your dog learns the value of checking in. (There is more information later in the chapter about when to decrease the number of times you give a treat.) However, at this point in training, be aware that your dog is learning one of two things: either that it's rewarding to pay attention to you no matter what else is going on, *or* that the best things in life have nothing to do with you, but lie in the smells on the ground or in watching the dog next door.

SIT AND DOWN

NO, I DON'T ALWAYS HAVE FOOD IN MY HAND This week continue working on sit and down, but begin to use what's called *intermittent reinforcement* for the times your dog sits when asked. That means you should give your dog a food reward for some of her correct responses, but not all. This is an important step in training, but is one that is often neglected by novices. Skipping this step—the gradual withdrawal of treats—can result in a dog who works only if you have goodies in your pocket, so be sure that you go out of your way to decide when to give your dog a food reward. Sit is relatively easy for dogs to do, so use it to practice decreasing the amount of food rewards you give your dog. Lying down on cue is a bit harder for dogs, so continue using food reinforcements 100% of the time for it, and begin your intermittent reinforcement for the sit cue only.

In a quiet environment, ask your dog to sit with either a verbal cue or a hand motion. Praise and give her a food reward from your other hand, and then ask again. If all goes well, give her praise and a treat for the second sit, and then immediately ask for a third one. This time don't give her a treat. Give her lots of verbal praise, but resist giving her a food reward. Go back to giving her both praise and a treat for the fourth repetition. Ask a fifth time, and withhold the treat and just praise her. Try one more, and this time give her the treat.

You get the idea: start by giving her a food treat, and then begin to intermix praise and treat with praise alone. The goal is to condition her to feel good when she does what she was asked, without having your pockets smelling like dried liver for the rest of your life. The trick is to know when you can start decreasing the number of treats you use. It's hard to provide a formula, because each dog is so different, but the following will help you decide when you can start intermittently dropping out treats. 1) The general rule is to start decreasing the number of times you give a treat when you think there's an 80% chance your dog will do what you asked. Some people suggest that you can start when you're willing to bet five dollars your dog will sit on cue. 2) Go back to 100% reinforcement any time the exercise is more difficult for your dog, such as when she's nervous, distracted or in a new place. 3) Most importantly, avoid the common mistake made by novices, of giving the dog a treat for every response for weeks and months, and then suddenly expecting the dog to perform for no food at all. In contrast, you can make amazing progress by decreasing the frequency of food rewards early on, when it's relatively easy for your dog to comply, but going back to 100% reinforcement whenever things get a bit more difficult.

THERE'S MORE TO LIFE THAN FOOD This is a good time to mention the importance of using reinforcements other than food. After all, none of us want to carry food in our pockets for the next fifteen years. Even if we did, dogs don't always want food as much as they want to chase a squirrel or roll in a cow pie. So start now to vary what you give your dog as a reinforcement for listening to you, using *play* and *petting* as well as food treats and praise. That way your dog will learn that doing what you ask makes her happy, so that attention and compliance become a habit.

The key to using play and petting successfully is to be sure you know what varieties of each your dog enjoys. As mentioned earlier, many dogs dislike being patted on top of their heads, so use your observational skills to decide what type of petting your dog really likes. Most dogs like chest, cheek and ear rubs, and some dogs can't get enough scratching above their tails, but many dogs would rather skip the massage altogether when they're in play mode. Lots of slap-happy labradors love vigorous and affectionate thumps, but be careful about breed stereotypes, because lots of labs prefer a softer touch. Every dog is different, so experiment

The goal is to condition your dog to feel good when she does what she was asked, without having your pockets smell like dried liver for the rest of your life.

a bit to see which type of touch makes your dog beg for more, and which type your dog walks away from.

Dogs also vary in how they like to play: some dogs love tug of war, others refuse to put that disgusting, slimy rope in their mouth no matter what. We'll consider different ways to play with your dog in a later chapter, but for now, remember that as you drop food out, you can add appropriate play and petting as valuable reinforcements. The more you mix and match reinforcements, the more likely your dog will do what you ask, whether she's hungry or not.

YOU STAY UP WHEN YOUR DOG GOES DOWN Continue 100% reinforcement for the more challenging lie down cue, but work on decreasing the amount of help you give your dog with the movements of your body. Your job this week is to decrease the amount of "prompting" you do to encourage your dog to lie down.[14] Begin by sitting or squatting beside your dog, and ask for a down with a clear verbal cue, followed by a sweep of the hand (with treat) down toward the ground. As before, praise and give a treat for all correct responses. Treat a good response, and then ask again by moving your hand only partway to the ground. Don't change too much too fast—go ahead and lure your dog's nose most of the way down, but stop about six inches above the ground.

Your goal is to change your position so that you can ask for a down while standing up straight, and sweeping your hand in a downward motion toward the ground.

If your dog lies down, give her lots of praise and an extra treat or two, and then try again with your hand a bit higher off the floor. As the days go on, try asking her to lie down while you are standing up, although you should still bend your knees and move your hand as close to the ground as needed for her to understand the cue. Avoid bending over at the waist toward your dog, or she will likely come to expect that movement as part of the cue. Your goal is to change your position so that you can ask for a down while standing up straight, and sweep your hand in a downward motion toward the ground. The trick is to gradually straighten up your own body so that you can signal her while standing up, and help her understand your visual cue without moving your hand all the way to the ground.

SWAP HANDS If things are going well, you can also experiment with

[14] Prompts are sounds or movements you make to help your dog do what you want—like tapping the ground to encourage your dog to lie down. The key to using prompts is to drop them out early on, so that the dog distinguishes them from the cue you are trying to teach.

moving the treat to your other hand. It helps if there is the scent of food on your cue hand, so handle the treat with both hands before you give the visual cue. Don't combine holding the treat in your other hand while you're working on standing up while you ask for a down—that's too many changes at once.

COME

INCREASE THE DISTANCE This week it's time to start calling your dog when you are a bit further away than before. Every additional five feet of distance between you and your dog increases the difficulty of the exercise, so continue to be thoughtful about the space between you and your dog when you call "come." Often dog lovers don't think about the distance between them and their dog as a variable, and set themselves up to fail by calling the dog when he is too far away for his level of training. You can avoid that this week by only calling your dog to come when he's less than twenty feet away. If he's farther away than that, simply walk toward him and call when you're closer. This seems to be surprisingly difficult for us to do—almost every novice dog trainer has to be encouraged to move across the floor toward their dog, rather than standing still and repeating themselves. Of course, no matter what the distance, continue to call only when he's not overly distracted by something else in the environment, and ensuring that he's really, really glad he came.

It's worth taking a moment to consider what we're asking of a dog when we call him to come to us. It seems so simple and basic to us—who could have a dog and not want him to come when called? It just seems like it is a part of having a good dog: You call, he comes running, simple as that. However, it's not simple at all if you think about it from your dog's perspective. There's nothing in the repertoire of a dog that would make it natural for him to turn around in mid-air and run to you joyfully just because you made a noise. For that reason, teaching come is different than teaching sit or lie down. Dogs sit and lie down on their own all the time; training involves getting them to do it on cue, not to do it in the first place. On the other hand, dogs don't pivot away from interesting things just because a pack member barks out "come right now." There's no equivalent in a dog pack to our come cue. Come to think about it, there isn't one in human society either. Do your children turn on a dime and dash to you breathlessly every time you call their name? Ever said "just a minute . . ." when someone said your name and you were concentrating on something else? Perhaps that's what your dog is saying when you call and he continues sniffing the ground. "Just a minute, be right there, but I just found a dead squirrel and it has worms in it!"

Think of teaching your dog to come like a difficult trick, in which you start with baby steps and gradually increase the difficulty. Remember that although dogs don't automatically come when called, they like to chase moving things, so don't forget to immediately move away from your dog after calling "come."

In summary, here's what you need to do to have a dog with a reliable recall: gradually increase the distance between you and your dog, spend *at least* three solid weeks calling come only when there are few other distractions, help your dog do the right thing by moving away from him, and shower him with praise, treats and play when he comes when called. Great reinforcements are like money in the bank—think of them as deposits you are making now that you can withdraw later, with interest. Avoid the common mistake of skimping on reinforcements when a dog does a great recall, and be as generous as you can so that he'll want to come the next time you call.

Think of teaching your dog to come when called like a difficult trick, in which you start with baby steps and gradually increase the difficulty.

HEEL

WALK SLOWLY AND IGNORE ALL INTERESTING THINGS? If dogs could talk, that's probably how they'd label heel. We may want our dogs to walk side-by-side with us, but it's not something that dogs naturally do. Dogs don't walk beside one another, shoulder to shoulder, like two best friends out for a Sunday stroll. Walking side-by-side may be something that we associate with friendship, but no matter how much our dogs love us, it's not a natural behavior for them. Even dogs who are the best of friends walk here, there and everywhere on their own— investigating the bounty of smells around them. You can teach dogs that it's fun to walk like a human (well, okay, not exactly) if you start by making it a game.

Start heel training by teaching your dog that it's fun to stay with you as you walk. Don't worry that this won't look much like a finished heel yet—keep the faith for the next few weeks and make heeling feel like play. You don't even want to use the word "heel" yet, not until you have gotten your dog in the habit of walking beside you at the same pace for at least a couple of strides.

Find a safe, quiet area where you can drop your dog's leash without any risk. Put a few tasty treats in your left hand[15] and keep the rest of the treats easily accessible. Show your dog the treats and stride away. This week, do everything you can to help your dog stay with you— you can slap your left leg, smooch or make clicking noises, speed up as if to run away, and/or wave the treat down by your left knee. If your dog has stayed with you after two or three strides, even if he's a bit behind you, give him praise and a treat from your left hand. If he hasn't, go back to him and put the treat within an inch of his nose. If he ignores it and goes back to sniffing the grass, go back inside and get a better treat or try in an area with fewer distractions.

Once your dog has been reinforced, walk a few steps in a different direction, doing what's needed to keep his attention. Reward him again if he's tried to stay with you, delivering the treat as he walks by your side. Your goal is to be so interesting that your dog can't help but want to walk beside you. One of the ways to do that is to vary your direction and speed— most of us walk too slowly to be interesting to our dogs, so speed up for a stride or two and see if that keeps your dog's attention. Try moving so unpredictably that your dog becomes riveted by your changes in speed and quick turns. Aimee and I call this, with apologies to half of the population, our "crazy woman" routine. Besides being fun and silly, it gives us lots of opportunities to reinforce our dogs for doing what we want.

Try this a couple of times a day, for very short periods of time—thirty or sixty seconds is plenty at this stage of training. As usual, only practice this when there are few distractions and you are sure that your dog is hungry for the goodies you've got in your pocket.

Start heel training by teaching your dog that it's fun to stay with you as you walk.

---

[15] Most people prefer their dogs to heel on the left side, so that's what we'll describe. It's fine to have your dog heel on the right if you'd rather, but once you pick a side, don't confuse your dog by switching back and forth.

STAY

If things went well during your "micro-stays" last week, it's time to increase the duration of your stays. We're not talking about asking your dog to stay for five minutes, or even for thirty seconds, but for two to four seconds. That paltry amount of time might seem silly, but it'll pay off in the long run. If you spend the first few weeks on stays that are no longer than a few seconds, you can start increasing their duration much more rapidly in the weeks to follow. It takes discipline for all of us to keep from asking for longer stays at this point, so focus on staying patient and continuing to build on success. Strong foundations are just as important in dog training as they are in houses, so don't get impatient and push the envelope at this point.

This week, ask your dog to sit as usual, saying "stay" with that quiet voice you worked on last week and flashing your dominant hand out like a traffic cop as you back up one or two steps. (Be sure that you are holding the treat in the hand you *aren't* using to signal the stay.) As you back up, consciously drop your cue hand, so that both of your arms are held loosely at the side. Look directly at your dog, staying still yourself for a count of one-one-thousand, two-one-thousand. Then rock forward, and with the underhanded motion you practiced last week, slip a treat in your dog's mouth. Rock back again no more than one or two small steps, and count one-one-thousand. If she's still staying in place, immediately release her with a quiet "okay" or "free." Remember to keep the release low key, even a bit boring, so that she doesn't anticipate the release, waiting for the fun to begin. The fun should come to her as she's staying, in the form of quiet praise and tasty treats, not when she gets up.

BODY BLOCKS Now that you're asking your dog to stay a little longer, even if it is only a few seconds, you need to be prepared to react if she gets up before you release her. The best way to do that is to counter her forward motion with one of your own. Watch her closely, and if she starts to get up, rock your body forward like a traffic cop stopping an oncoming car. You can even move your hands up and out, as if to block the space in front of her. Dogs are very responsive to forward motion, and sometimes even the smallest movement can keep them from getting up, especially if you do it quickly, before the dog has started to walk away. This method works best, by the way, if your dog

If you spend the first few weeks on stays that are no longer than a few seconds, you can start increasing their duration much more rapidly in the weeks to follow.

is most likely to move toward you, so set up your sessions such that any potential distractions will be behind you, not behind your dog.

Think of these body blocks as a dance between you and your dog, in which you are primed to counter her forward motion with just enough of your own to stop her. Watch her carefully for the slightest sign that she is hesitating in response, and instantly reward that hesitation by backing off to your original position. Some dogs are very sensitive to body blocks, so you need to be careful not to overdo them. Lean forward enough to stop your dog's forward motion, and then rock backward the instant she settles back down. If you lean forward too much or for too long (the most common mistake with body blocks) you can put too much pressure on your dog, and inadvertently punish her for trying to stay in place. Those of you with overly-exuberant dogs are no doubt guffawing right now, because the last thing you need to worry about is hurting Rambo's feelings. What's important is to observe your dog carefully and use just enough body language to settle your particular dog back down.

If you miss the magic moment, and your dog is already up and walking away, simply go to her, put a treat right beside her nose and lure her back to where she started. *Visually* ask for a sit and stay, count one or two seconds and then give her a treat for staying before you release her. Don't worry when your dog breaks the stay and gets three strides away before you can stop her—it'll happen. Just stay calm and quiet and lure her back to where you want her, and use your visual cues to ask her to sit and stay again. Do all you can to avoid repeating the verbal cue, because that's the one you want to work the first time, every time.

WHO'S REINFORCING YOU?

We said earlier that dog training isn't just about dogs, and this week it's especially important to think about the animal at the other end of the leash. You've been continually reinforcing your dog—praising, handing out treats—but who's reinforcing you? Yes, it's gratifying to watch your dog make progress, and that in itself feels good, but you'd be wise to do a little extra for yourself this week. You're working on your own behavior as much as you are your dog's behavior and that effort is worth reinforcing. Keep in mind that it takes 21 to 28 days to

Dogs are very responsive to forward motion, and sometimes even the smallest movement can keep them from getting up, especially if you do it quickly, before the dog has started to walk away.

rewire the human brain to learn a new habit. However, unless they consciously avoid it, people tend to go back to their old habits after only two weeks of working on a new one—and end up back where they started. You can avoid this by going out of your way to reinforce yourself for the time and effort you've been putting in, especially during this third week.

We want you to keep up the good work, so go out of your way to do something special for yourself.

Have some fun thinking about what would be a good self-reinforcement and how to go about providing it. You could try reinforcing yourself during every training session, just like you do your dog (M & M's anyone?). You could go for something big that you anticipate all week long, like a huge ice cream sundae or a massage at the spa. Remember that, just like your dog, it's YOU who gets to decide what is truly reinforcing!

WEEKLY SUMMARY

• NO Teach your dog a word that means "uh uh, that's not allowed here" by saying it in a low-pitched voice and reinforcing him for turning away from the object of his misbehavior. Avoid using a high volume to stop your dog—rather, say the word and then lure him away with a treat. As soon as you can, drop out the lure and give him a feast of treats for stopping to your voice alone.

• SIT Continue asking your dog to sit with either a visual or a verbal cue, working toward your dog responding equally well to one or the other. Don't hesitate to use a word followed by a hand cue if your dog is distracted. Begin using intermittent reinforcement when you are confident that your dog is going to respond correctly to your signal. Use 100% reinforcement in any new or overly distracting environment.

• DOWN Give your dog a treat every time she lies down, but start decreasing the amount of movement you make with your body to lure her to the ground. Put the treat in the other hand, and try a session in which your cue hand only goes partway to the ground. Give her extra treats if she lies down to your modified visual cue.

• ATTENTION GAME At least two or three times this week, take your dog and some extra tasty treats to a distracting environment (on leash, of course). Don't show him that you have treats, unless he's easily distracted by the scents on the ground (we're thinking Beagle here!). Let him look and sniff to his heart's content, but every time he happens to look at you, give him a treat.

• COME This week begin to ask your dog to come when you are a bit farther away, perhaps from ten to twenty feet away. Remember to avoid repeating yourself if she doesn't respond. Rather, go to her and lure her in the right direction, then treat and praise, and try again.

• STAY Begin to *gradually* lengthen the amount of time you ask her to stay, asking for stays only slightly longer than last week. Try for stays that are 2 to 4 seconds long. Use body blocks if your dog starts to get up, moving forward just enough to block her own forward motion, and backing up to take off the pressure as soon as she rocks backward.

• NAME GAME, FOUR ON THE FLOOR Continue to reinforce your dog for looking at you when you say his name, and continue last week's exercises to encourage Chester to keep his paws on the ground when company comes. Remember to ask the visitor to say "sit," but be ready with treats as soon as your dog complies. It's relatively easy to find help for this exercise—it's a rare person who doesn't enjoy helping you out, especially when you say "Would you mind helping me teach my dog to be polite to visitors?"

• REINFORCE YOURSELF No fooling, you need reinforcement too! Take this part seriously, and go out of your way to reward yourself for all your hard work. This is the toughest week in many ways—you've been working hard (even if you've only done some of what's been suggested!)—AND, this is the week that people naturally start going back to their old habits. So hang in there, and buy yourself a present on us. Well, not exactly—invoices will not be accepted, but you get the idea . . .

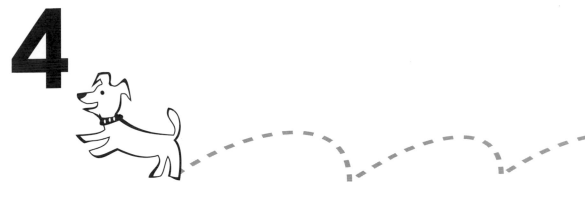

WHOSE HOUSE IS THIS ANYWAY?

I know you love your dog. But if you love your dog, you'll do him no favors by catering to him or providing him with no boundaries. Dogs need to feel secure to be truly happy; and that means they need to be able to count on you be in charge. This does NOT mean that you need to "get dominance" over your dog: that's a fallacy we'll discuss in the next section. It does mean that your dog needs you to be a benevolent leader. Dogs need us to provide loving and fair boundaries on their behavior, in the same way that children need the same thing from good parents and good teachers. Dogs are happiest, and we are happiest with them, if they are taught to be patient and polite, rather than learning to get what they want by being pushy and rude.

Teaching manners is easier with some dogs than others, just as it is with children. Even as puppies, some dogs have little tolerance for frustration, and can lose their tempers quickly if they don't get what they want. These dogs might be a bit of a challenge, but they are the ones who most need to learn that patience pays off. Your dog, no matter what his personality, has been learning some of this already: stay, for example, is a wonderful lesson in patience and emotional control. As you progress in teaching stay, you can work your way up to longer stays —first three seconds, then five, ten… Eventually, in a few months, you can ask your dog to lie down and stay for fifteen to thirty minutes while you eat dinner or watch a television show.

Two additional exercises, introduced this week, also teach dogs the value of patient, polite behavior. *Wait* means "please pause for a moment," and is an exceptionally useful cue. You can use it to prevent your dog from knocking you over when you open the door, to keep your dog in the car until you attach his leash and when he's gotten too

Dogs are happiest, and we are happiest with them, if they are taught to be patient and polite.

far ahead of you at the dog park. *Leave it*, which means "sorry, you can't have that right now" is equally useful, whether you've just dropped the Thanksgiving turkey on the kitchen floor or you notice that Fido is about to roll in a dead fish. Both of these exercises teach impulse control, a highly valuable commodity in any member of the family.

There are many ways to ensure that your dog isn't getting reinforced for being rude. Perhaps the best question to ask is: who is the *actor*, and who is the *reactor* in your household? Do you pet your dog every time he asks for it—or is the word "demand" a better description of his behavior? We're not saying you shouldn't pet your dog whenever you feel like it—but you should do it when *you* feel like it, not because you've been trained by your dog to pet him on demand. Does one of your dogs always push in front of your other dog and end up hogging the attention? If so, then the pushy one is getting reinforced for being rude, which is the opposite of what he should be learning.

This week, think about the interactions you have with your dog when you're not "training," and ask yourself what your behavior is teaching your dog. If you discover, as many of us do, that we are inadvertently teaching our dogs to be pushy and demanding because they are so darned cute, then it's time to turn the tables. Of course, you'll want to role model being polite yourself. For example, if your dog comes up and nudges your arm for petting, respond by quietly asking for a sit. Then give him a pet—for sitting politely, not for nudging your arm. If Max pushes your other dog out of the way to soak up attention, ask him to lie down and stay for a moment, and *then* give him attention. You'll find it takes some energy at first—it's so easy to stroke your dog's head while you're reading the paper every time your dog slaps a paw in your lap—but it won't take long before it becomes second nature to reinforce polite behavior rather than rudeness. Before you know it, patient and polite behavior will become second nature to your dog too.

THE DOMINANCE FALLACY

"You've got to get dominance over your dog!" People having been telling us this for decades, but here's the deal: No you don't. Does your dog need to learn boundaries? Yes. Does your dog need to be patient and polite, and to respect you as well as love you? Yes. However, the oft-repeated advice that you "need to get dominance over your dog" is fraught with problems. First of all, it often leads to the belief that one needs to use coercion to force dogs into submission. Owners are advised to do "alpha roll-overs," pushing dogs into submissive postures as a way of establishing that the human is the pack leader. This is supposedly based on wolf behavior, in which subordinate pack members are rolled over on their backs by pack leaders to enforce their dominance. It's true that rolling over and showing one's belly is an appeasement gesture, but it is initiated by the subordinate. Higher status wolves don't grab others by the ruff and flip them over on their backs. Besides, dogs aren't wolves, and neither, for that matter, are we. Forcing dogs into physical "submission" *can* be very effective—at teaching your dog to be afraid of you, at eliciting defensive aggression, or at role modeling that one gets what one wants by being violent.

It's not that social status isn't relevant in dog society, but it's relevant a small amount of the time, just as it is in human interactions. If you struggled with algebra in high school it probably wasn't because you didn't respect your teacher—you either didn't like math, or you preferred doing something besides solving quadratic equations. You don't forget your lines in a speech because you don't respect your audience—you forgot what to say because you were nervous, or you didn't practice enough (or both). Dogs don't do what we ask of them for many of the same reasons that we don't always do what we're asked—in both cases we may be confused, scared, or motivated to do something else. However, it's very common for owners to assume that their dogs are purposefully challenging their authority when they don't do everything they're asked, whether it's not coming when called or being polite to visitors. We even call it "disobedience," when more often it should be called "miscommunication" or "stage fright." Keep that in mind as you work with your dog. Everyone will be happiest if you come across as the benevolent leader, parent, or teacher rather than an authoritarian dictator.

You'll all be happiest if you come across as the benevolent leader, parent, or teacher rather than an authoritarian dictator.

THIS WEEK'S EXERCISES

THE ATTENTION GAME

Play the attention game at least three or four times this week, whether it's in the backyard, at dog training class or on a neighborhood walk. Avoid trying this if your dog is twenty feet ahead of you on a Flexi lead—that's too difficult for your dog at this stage of training. However, you could try stopping and standing still for a minute or two when you're on a walk, reinforcing your dog if she turns her head to look at you.

Focus your attention on two events: the movement of your dog's head as it turns toward you, and the action of speaking your praise word.

This is also a good time to practice the timing of your praise. Focus your attention on two events: the movement of your dog's head as it begins to turn toward you, and the action of speaking your praise word. Ask yourself: how much time elapsed between those two events? Concentrate on decreasing the time interval between your dog starting to move her head toward you, and her hearing the word "Good!" Precision timing is an aspect of dog training that sounds so simple, but it takes practice to perfect.[16] Most beginners let as much as a second go by between the dog's action and their response. That might not seem like much, but a second is enough time for lots of things to happen, each of which could interfere with your dog relating your praise word to the movement of her head. You can illustrate this yourself by saying "one-one-thousand" out loud. As you do, move as many ways as you can while you're speaking. Most of us can manage at least five or ten tiny movements within that seemingly miniscule period of time. Each of those movements could mean something to your dog, so you can see why, to behaviorists (and dogs), one entire second is a long time indeed.

With that in mind, see if you can get your own response time down to about a quarter of a second. As soon as your dog's head begins to turn, you should begin to say "Good!" Don't worry that it will take a bit more time to get the treat into her mouth, because you've already conditioned her to link your praise with a treat (aren't you glad you didn't skip that section?).

[16] Using a clicker as a secondary reinforcement can be a great way to practice and perfect good timing.

Good timing is one of the distinguishing characteristics of a good dog trainer, and if you can improve your timing you'll be heads and shoulders ahead of most dog owners. Most importantly, your dog will be less confused, and if she could, would tell the world how happy she is to have an owner who makes so much sense.

FOUR ON THE FLOOR

GET REAL This week try to set up training sessions in which "real" visitors come over to the house and help teach good manners to your dog. It's important to pick people who will enjoy helping you out, but who won't hinder your efforts by encouraging your dog to jump up while saying "Oh, it's okay, I don't mind!" We all have friends like that (sigh), so be sure that your friends are enrolled in helping you out. Your job is to make sure your visitors are well versed in their role: to ask for a sit as soon as the door opens or as the dog approaches, to stand still while you treat if the dog sits, or to turn away and leave if the dog jumps up.

There are times this just won't be practical. If Fed Ex is at the door, or grumpy Uncle Charles is coming over, don't hesitate to put your little darling in another room. Bad habits are as hard to break in dogs as they are in people, so try to prevent problematic experiences at the door when you can. On the other hand, don't worry too much if your adolescent dog bounces off of your insurance agent's shoulders when the kids opened the door before you have time to react. Stuff happens, even to the best of trainers, and a couple of chaotic experiences at the door aren't going to ruin all your hard work.

JACKPOTS AND THE AUTOMATIC SIT This is also the time to take one step closer to your ultimate goal: a dog who sits automatically, without a cue, when greeting visitors. Begin with your usual routine in which a visitor asks for sit, and you praise and treat. Repeat that, right away, one more time. Repeat again, but this time have the visitor approach, stand still and remain silent for a few seconds. This will give your dog a chance to sit down on his own accord. That's the goal—to have your dog sit on his own when he's greeting someone.

The first time that your dog sits on his own to a visitor, give him what trainers call a *jackpot*. Jackpots are *five or ten* treats given rapidly and sequentially, and they have an immediate impact on a dog's response. Most dogs appear to be joyfully stunned at the profusion of goodies raining down upon them, hopefully thinking something like: "What did I do to deserve this?" Hand the treats out rapidly, but one at a time, while enthusiastically praising your brilliant student. "GOOD!" *Treat*. "You are SO smart!" *Treat*. "I'm SO proud of you." *Treat*. "Wow, what a dog! *Treat*, etc. etc. Don't make the mistake of giving him a handful of treats all at once, it doesn't seem to have the same impact if the treats are gulped down in one swallow.

Don't worry if an automatic sit doesn't happen the first time you try. Lots of dogs won't be ready until the second or third session. It will happen more quickly if you ask him to sit several times in a row in the same context with the same person, and then wait a few seconds for him to do it on his own. If he doesn't sit on his own after you've waited for three to four seconds, don't worry. Just have the visitor leave and come back a minute later, and this time have the visitor ask for the sit as before. You can try for the automatic sit in the next session.

Most dogs will offer at least one "auto-sit" within a few sessions, and it's the most important step you can take to teach manners with company to a dog. Be prepared for your dog to alternate between jumping up, sitting on cue, and sitting by himself for several months. Your goal is to see a gradual decrease in jumping up and an increase in auto-sits over time. This is a tough exercise for lots of dogs, so be patient and don't expect this to get turned around in a week or two.

HEEL

LET YOUR DOG DECIDE Last week we advised you to smooch, clap your hands, or do anything else necessary to encourage your dog to stay close to you. This week you're going to do something different. This new exercise will lead to that relaxed, seamless heel we'd all like, but be forewarned—at this stage it won't look anything like a finished heel. It's called the Follow Game, and it is a wonderful way to teach your dog the value of walking beside you.

This time, you're not going to "help" your dog catch up with you— you're going to remain silent and walk in big circles around your dog.

The idea is to teach your dog that it's fun to pay attention to you, and that wonderful things happen if he decides *on his own* to join up with you. There are two reasons this is important. As you remember, dogs learn faster and perform best if they initiate the behavior themselves. Additionally, although it is useful in the beginning stages of training to use claps or smooches (or "prompts") to keep your dog beside you, you eventually want your dog to respond to the word "heel,' not to the body language you used at first to encourage him to walk beside you.

Start in an area where it is 100% safe for your dog to be off leash. You could also use a light, long line and ask a friend to hold onto the end to ensure that your dog doesn't take off. Ideally the area will not be so interesting that your dog is lost in chipmunk tracks and raccoon poop—try to find an area where your dog has already done all the sniffing he needs to do, perhaps a flat, plain piece of grass or a quiet basement. Be sure you're loaded up with lots of tasty goodies that are easy for you to dispense, and then ask your dog to sit and give him a treat. If the leash is still on at this point, snap it off and stride away as if late for a meeting. Don't do anything to try to get your dog to follow you, just walk away. Walk in big circles around your dog, perhaps ten to fifteen feet away and wait for that magic moment when he decides to catch up to you. Resist the urge to lure your dog with the treat, to call, clap, or, for that matter, to pay any attention to your dog whatsoever.

This is harder than it sounds; at least half of the participants in training classes find themselves unable to walk away from their dog without adding in some kind of encouragement. Stay focused on walking purposefully by yourself—this game is about your dog making his own decision, not about helping him to do the right thing. We want him to decide that there's a good reason to choose you over everything else in the environment, so do your best to ignore him completely as you stride around him.

Watch him out of the corner of your eye, and the instant he approaches within a foot or so, stop walking and give him lots of praise and several wonderful treats. Now try walking away again, watching for the next time he moves toward you. As soon as it feels like he's "caught up," treat him again, and then resume walking.

Stay focused on walking purposefully by yourself – this game is about your dog making his own decision, not about helping him to do the right thing.

If you've walked four or five circles around your dog and he's completely ignored you, you can try one of the following:

~ Try walking within a foot or two of your dog, or standing in front of him to get his attention. Praise and treat any kind of attention from your dog, then walk away again, structuring your circle so that you pass close to your dog at one point in the circle.

~ Increase your pace, and/or vary it. Dogs are stimulated by faster movements, and often ignore what to them is the unbelievably slow pace of their humans.

~ If none of this works, go back to your dog, show him a treat by putting it right beside his nose, and lure him—like a donkey following a carrot—for a couple of steps. Then give him the treat. Next time, try an area that is a bit less distracting and reconsider your choice of treats.

If, on the other hand, your dog has decided you are indeed the best game in town and has begun walking beside you, liberally reinforce him as he walks beside you. If you find him dancing around you rather than staying on one side, you can use a treat as a lure to keep him in place.

LEAVE IT

"Leave it" is a new cue, and it's a handy signal for any dog owner to have. Leave it means "please ignore whatever it is that you are looking at"—be it a filthy fast-food wrapper in the gutter, a dead bird, or another dog looking for a fight. It's similar to "no" in that it is designed to stop your dog from doing something she shouldn't, but it means "not now," rather than "not ever." When my new pup starts to chase the cat I say "no," because he is learning that he should never chase the cat, no matter what. However, there are plenty of times when it's fine for him to sniff something lying in the grass, but if it's something that might be bad for him, I'll say "leave it." It's a fine distinction, but it might help you communicate more clearly—and that's always a good thing.

The beauty of teaching leave it is that it allows you to calmly and quietly tell your dog what you'd like her to do: to stop focusing on something and await further instructions. You can use it to avoid a potentially

The beauty of teaching 'leave it' is that it allows you to calmly and quietly tell your dog what you'll like her to do: to stop focusing on something and await further instructions.

dangerous dog or to keep Chester away from a dropped pork chop on the kitchen floor. (Warning: if you teach this step-by-step you just might end up with a dog who is so responsive that she'll stop just inches away from a sirloin steak. Once that happens, your friends will be so impressed they'll ask you to train their dog, and then how are you going to get anything done?)

Start with two treats, one in each hand—a "low-value" treat (perhaps an inexpensive dog biscuit made mostly of corn or wheat) and a "high-value" treat like a piece of chicken or liver. Go to a quiet area with your dog, and hold the good treat behind your back. Show her the low-value treat which is enclosed in your other hand, but don't let her have it. It works best to have a biscuit small enough to enclose in your fist, such that your dog can smell it, but not get it in her mouth. Say "leave it" like a statement of fact (don't ask your dog a question here, or you might not like the answer!), and watch your dog carefully. Most dogs will sniff and smell your hand—some will even paw at it to get at the treat. Wait it out, ignoring all your dog's efforts to get at the treat. Eventually, sometimes within just a few seconds, your dog will take her attention off your fist, and either look up at you or in another direction. Using that lightning-fast timing you've been practicing, immediately praise and give her the high-value treat from the *other hand*.

Repeat this exercise several times, always holding the low-value treat in one hand and the high-value one behind your back. Don't extend this to food or other treasures that your dog finds on the floor outside of a training session this week. That is a completely different context to your dog, and trying it now will compromise the foundation you are building. Next week we'll start with food on the floor, and work our way up to the graduate school of leave it—a rotten fish on the beach that your dog finds while walking twenty feet ahead of you—but she's no more ready for that stage now than most of us are ready to compete in the Olymics.

WAIT

This is an extremely useful signal that can prevent your dog from knocking you over while dashing out the door. It can also teach your dog the value of being patient and polite, and might someday even save his life. Wait differs from the stay cue in that it means "pause and don't move forward" rather than "sit or lie down in place." Aimee and I use it most often when we open the car door, aware as we are of at least two tragedies in which dogs leapt out into traffic when a car door swung open. It's also useful if you have more than one dog. Groups of dogs can compete to see who gets out the door first, sometimes with so much exuberance you are reminded of why clipping is illegal in football. Sometimes the pack ends up in a squabble because dog A ran into dog B and dog B didn't appreciate it and everyone is so aroused and excited they replicate the canine equivalent of "I went to a fight and a hockey game broke out."

In addition to the benefits listed above, wait is amazingly easy to teach, so it's well worth your effort. Start by putting your dog on a leash, and walking to the door you usually use to go on a walk. No need for treats here—getting to go outside is the reinforcement your dog wants most. Now, move yourself so that you are standing between the dog and the door, facing your dog with your back to the door. If your dog is right on top of the door or within inches of you, use the body blocks you learned in the stay exercise, and gently move him away from the door itself. You need your dog to be at least two or three feet back from the doorway for this to work. Once your dog is moved back from the door a few feet, back yourself up to the door.

Wait is amazingly easy to teach, so it's well worth your effort.

Turn your body partially toward the door and say "wait" in a clear voice, using a quiet, confident tone. Open the door about a foot or so, keeping your eye on your dog. Most dogs try to dash out the instant a door is opened, so be ready to block your dog by stepping in front of him and blocking access to the great outdoors. Think of it as managing the space around your dog—the message is "that space is not available." If your dog pauses the slightest bit and you no longer feel that he's about to dash outside, step to the side a half a step. If he still stays in place for just a microsecond, say "okay" and let him trot outside. The easiest mistake to make at this point is to wait too long, and miss the chance to reinforce your dog for hesitating. Concentrate on this split-second timing you've been working on, and you'll be amazed at how much progress you can make in just a few sessions. If expect your dog to wait for too long, you'll set him up to fail, and you'll both get frustrated.

Teaching wait is a great test of your timing and your ability to read your dog, and if you can master it you can bring your training skills up a notch. Your dog has a lot to gain as well: he'll learn that the way to get what he wants is to be patient and polite, rather than throwing himself forward in a flurry of arousal when he wants something. In the early stages it helps to go back inside and repeat this once or twice before you go on your walk (or your play session in the backyard), but don't do this over and over again. A few times will go a long way toward helping your dog learn impulse control.

One word of caution: guard against doing what is oh-so-natural, which is to use the leash rather than trusting your body to stop your dog. Even if we don't mean to do it, our innate response is to pull back on the leash if it's in our hands. You want your dog to learn impulse control himself, and to learn it without getting hurt. Leash jerks can hurt dogs and in the long run can cause structural problems—dogs weren't designed to have their necks jerked any more than we were. Leash corrections can also teach dogs to be anxious about going in and out of doors, so work hard to keep the leash loose and let your body do the talking. In classes we often have the trainer hold the leash, so that the student can concentrate on moving his or her body to control the dog, rather than using the leash. If you find that this is an issue for you, you can have a friend hold the leash or you can tie the leash to your belt if you have a little dog (we are NOT responsible for people who attach their bodies to a Great Dane). Of course, you can work on this off-leash if your dog is about to move into an area that is well fenced.

WEEKLY SUMMARY

- **ATTENTION GAME** Play the attention game at least three or four times this week, focusing on the timing of your praise. Work toward saying "good dog" within a quarter of a second of the turning of your dog's head.

- **FOUR ON THE FLOOR, AUTO SITS AND JACKPOTS** This week have "real" visitors come over to the house, but ensure that your friends are clear about what you want. Their job is to say "sit" as the door opens or as they approach your dog. If your dog sits, give him a treat. If he doesn't, the visitor should turn and walk away. Create training sessions in which your dog is likely to sit all by himself, by having the visitor ask for a sit several times in a row, and then repeating the exercise without saying sit. If Fido sits on his own, jackpot him with five to ten treats in a row.

- **HEEL** This week play a game in which your dog gets reinforced for making a choice to join up with you. Take his off leash in a safe place or use a long line if necessary. Show him the treats in your hand, and stride away as if you have places to go, people to meet. Don't call, smooch or lure him in any way—let him decide on his own what he'd like to do. Walk around him in big circles, coming closer to him if you think you need to, and wait for him to move toward you. As soon as he's within a foot or so, stop, praise and treat generously. Then stride away again, continuing to reinforce him for choosing to join up. If he ignores you, don't call to him, but go back to him and show him the treats again. Try walking right by him, perhaps dangling the treats in the air over his nose. As soon as you can, drop out all encouragements, and let him make his own choices about what to do.

- **LEAVE IT** Put a low-value treat in one hand and high-value treat in the other. Hide the good one behind your back, say "leave it" like a statement of fact and then move the low-value treat, enclosed in your fist, to her nose. Let her do whatever she wants (except, perhaps, chew your hand to shreds) while you watch for the instant that she gives up and takes her attention off the treat. Even if she turns her head away for a millisecond, reinforce that response by immediately praising and giving her the treat from your other hand. Repeat this four to five times in a row, one or two times a day.

• WAIT Teach your dog impulse control and manners at the door by asking him to pause when you say "wait." Start by going to the door you usually use for walks and outdoor play, and move yourself so that you are between the dog and the door. If he's pressing against you or the door, use body blocks to move him back from the doorway two or three feet. Go back toward the door, say "wait" and open the door. Be ready to block him from going outside by moving into the doorway before he can go through it. As soon as he stops and you feel he's stopped leaning forward as if he's about to charge through, say "okay" and let him through.

• COME, SIT, DOWN, and the NAME GAME Keep working on these exercises, following the instructions from last week. You've introduced a lot of new material this week, so if anything, lower your expectations a bit for these exercises, but try to intersperse each of these cues throughout the day as time allows.

5

PLAY! PLAY! PLAY!

ALL PLAY IS NOT EQUAL How you play with your dog (and how you don't) makes a big difference in how your dog behaves, both in and out of play sessions. Play can enhance your relationship, increase your dog's willingness to do what you ask, teach emotional control, and in general make life a lot more fun. That's a pretty impressive list of good things. However, anything with the power to do that much good can also do harm, and serious harm at that. Inappropriate play can teach bad habits and create dogs who are emotionally out of control. We don't want to see you in our office, your heart broken over a bite whose origin was in inappropriate play, so think carefully about how you play with your dog. Just a small amount of information, if taken seriously, can ensure that play sessions remain joyful and constructive.

A WORD ABOUT TOYS Many games with your dog will involve toys, but be thoughtful when you're shopping for dog toys. Some of the toys on the market aren't safe for dogs, so choose carefully. Your best bet is to buy toys at a pet store or from a pet catalog, rather than picking something up in the supermarket. At least some of your dog's toys should be made of hollow, indestructible rubber into which you can stuff food. There's nothing like a smear of peanut butter to convince your dog that the new toy you bought is better than your ankle. Experiment a bit to see what type of toys your dog likes best. Some dogs love balls (including tennis balls, but be sure they don't chew the fuzz off, it's bad for their teeth), others love hollow, bouncy toys like Kongs and Busy Buddies. Many dogs love soft, plush toys, although some love to rip them into shreds the minute you cut off the tag. Squeakers inside of toys are especially attractive (and potentially dangerous) to a lot of dogs. If that's true of your dog, don't leave plush or squeaky toys

Play can enhance your relationship, increase your dog's willingness to do what you ask, teach emotional control, and in general make life a lot more fun.

around the house when you're gone—your dog might start eating them rather than playing with them.

Encourage your dog to play by herself by stuffing hollow toys with smears of tasty food, and letting her lick the food out at her leisure. Check out the interactive toys on the market that can entertain your dog for a long time—many of them have strategically placed holes that allow pieces of kibble to fall out as your dog manipulates them. You can also encourage your dog to play with toys by having a large number of them in reserve, but only leaving three or four of them available at the same time. That way you can rotate in some "new" toys every week, even though you bought them months ago.

Although all dogs should have toys they can play with by themselves, the best kind of play is interactive play with you.

Although all dogs should have toys they can play with by themselves, the best kind of play is interactive play with you. It's not only fun for both of you, it's full of "teachable moments" that make your dog more responsive and better able to control being emotionally aroused. It's also a great way to enhance the bond between you and your dog. Of course, you get out what you put in—being exuberant and playful yourself will go a long way toward motivating a somewhat inhibited dog.

TEACH YOUR DOG TO FETCH

THE BEAUTY OF FETCH Fetch games are a wonderful way to exercise your dog, without having to hike five miles yourself before you get your first cup of morning coffee. You can stand in the backyard drinking a latte while your dog runs his tail off—at least you can if your dog brings the ball back so you can throw it again. The phrase "brings it back" is the key here. Lots of people say "Oh yes, my dog loves to fetch. He just doesn't bring the ball back." Not to put too fine a point on it, but that's called chasing, not fetching. However, any dog that will chase after a ball can be taught to bring it back, so take heart if your dog only has chasing in his repertoire.

THE FOUNDATION OF FETCH In an area with few distractions, start by waving the ball in front of your dog. It's usually the movement that interests most dogs, not the object. When Chief is focused on the ball, toss it only four or five feet away.[17] If Chief trots over and puts his mouth around it, that's great, but resist the urge to say "Good

---

[17] Most people throw it too far at the beginning, so save those over-handed baseball throws for later, when your dog has learned the basics.

Boy!" Lots of dogs drop the ball as soon as you say something, so keep your mouth shut and let your hands do the talking. Clap your hands together as if applauding and start running away from your dog. That will encourage him to move toward you with the ball in his mouth. Don't worry if he doesn't bring it all the way; even a few feet of fetching is worth lots of encouragement.

If he drops the ball after bringing it even part of the way, pick it up and *immediately* toss it a second time. Don't ask for him to sit before you throw it again—that won't reinforce him for bringing the ball back and might even feel like punishment to him. Neither does it help to clasp the ball to your bosom and say "Good Dog!" At this point, dogs just want the ball back, so use it as the reinforcement for fetching. Throw the ball the instant that you get it, and clap and run backward as soon as he takes it up in his mouth.

Repeat this a few times, but be careful about asking for too much too soon. Don't worry if your young dog loses interest after three or four tosses, it's common at this stage of training, especially when playing fetch outside. Gradually, over a period of months, throw the ball more often, ending either before your dog gets bored with the game or before he gets too tired. If your dog fetches five times in row, but on a later toss fails to chase after the ball, no problem. Game over. Don't coax and plead, just walk away. Otherwise you're being taught to fetch the ball yourself, and be forewarned: dogs are really, really good at teaching humans to retrieve!

TAG, I'M IT! Dogs are also good at teaching humans to chase them. The instructions above may be irrelevant to you, because your dog returns with the ball, but won't release it. When you reach toward the ball, Chief dashes off, eyes shining. Dogs adore chase games, especially if they're the ones being chased, and they are brilliant at teaching humans how to play. Dogs are consistent, persistent, and very, very observant, so be aware that unless you pay attention, you're going to be the student! Here's what the "chase me" section would look like if dogs wrote training books:

> Run back to your human with the ball in your mouth, and get just close enough that she has to lean forward a bit and stretch out her arm to try to take the ball out of your mouth. Wait until

Don't ask for him to sit before you throw it again — that won't reinforce him for bringing the ball back.

the very last instant, and then bolt backwards one or two feet. Guard against moving too far away and losing her attention — you want to move just far enough away to encourage her to reach out her arm again. Continue this routine until you tire of it yourself or your human begins to make loud, bark-like noises . . .

If this sounds familiar, read this next paragraph carefully. When your dog arrives at your feet with the ball locked in his mouth, turn away from him as if you have no interest in playing anymore. If he counters by moving around to stay in front of you, teasing you with the ball, keep turning away from him—even walking away a few steps. Playing hard to get works on dogs as well as on humans—most dogs will eventually drop the ball if you turn the tables on them. When Chief finally does open his mouth, be ready to pick up the ball and throw it. Throw it as if it were burning a hole in your hands—every millisecond that you hold onto the ball looks like hoarding to your dog. After many repetitions, most dogs get better and better at dropping the ball at your feet—having learned that holding on to the ball ends the game, and giving it up keeps the game going.

Hundreds of dogs turn into great retrievers when their owners perfected this method—but then, nothing works with all dogs. If it doesn't work with yours you can try one of the following: 1) Take two or three balls out with you, and tease your dog with the second one when he brings the first one back. As soon as he opens his mouth to drop the first ball, throw the second one. Start saying "drop" before you wave the second ball, and eventually your dog will open his mouth to the word all by itself, and you can phase out the "backup ball." 2) Alternatively, you could throw this book across the lawn as if it were a ball, and let your dog chew it up.

BALL? WHAT BALL Ah, but what of the dogs who won't chase after a ball at all? If your dog has no interest in a ball at all, try using a hollow toy with food tucked inside. Let your dog sniff the food and then toss the toy only a foot or two away. Don't even think about fetch training at this point—your goal is to get your dog to track a moving, inanimate object, to visually follow it in space, to go over to it and to open his mouth around it. Let your dog lay down with the toy and lick or chew to his heart's content. Once he's consistently attending to an object, try tossing one with no food inside and encouraging him to "take it" as described earlier in the chapter. Once he'll follow it and pick it up in his mouth you can start with the early stages of fetch training. This exercise has turned some dogs into retrievers, but it's important to know that not all dogs are interested in playing ball, even if the word "retriever" is in their breed name. There is a strong genetic component to fetching, and if your dog doesn't want to play, then find other games. After all, if it's not fun for all the participants, it's not really play, is it?

TAKE IT, DROP IT

THE MOST PRACTICAL OF GAMES "Take it" and "drop it" are wonderful cues to teach your dog. Not only are they helpful during object play, but they can also be used to teach your dog to willingly drop something she shouldn't have, whether it's your reading glasses or a moldy food wrapper she found in the gutter. The key to making this game practical is to teach dogs that drop it is the flip side of take it, and that both cues are part of a fun, silly game. Without any training, the words "drop it" are just meaningless noises to dogs. A common mistake made by novice dog owners is to yell "DROP IT!" before the dog knows what it means, and then feel frustrated when the dog doesn't respond. Ironically, a stern voice from an owner makes some dogs clench their teeth together even tighter, and can end up inadvertently teaching a dog that "drop it" means "stand still and hang on to whatever you have, as tightly as you can." Whoops. Probably not what the owner had in mind. You can avoid this by being proactive rather than reactive. Here's how:

Start by palming a tasty little treat in one hand, but don't show it to your dog. Pick up one of your dog's favorite toys, and wave it around in front of her with the other hand. As she opens her mouth to grab it, say "take it!" Praise her once she has it firmly in her mouth, but then move the treat that you've cleverly concealed in your other hand to her nose as you say drop it. Most dogs will sniff the treat, drop what's in their mouth and take the treat. Praise her as she eats the treat and pick up the toy in your other hand. After she's finished her snack, show her that you don't have any more food in your hands. Now wave the toy a foot or so from her face to get her interested in it again. Just before you think she's going to open her mouth, say "take it!" again. If she does, give her lots of praise and play with her and the toy, either tossing it for her to chase, or playing a short game of tug of war. Repeat this several times a day, incorporating it into your regular play sessions.

Resist the universal urge to go from the take it/drop it equivalent of kindergarten to something more akin to graduate school. It can take weeks or months to create a foundation that will result in a dog dropping a dead bird just because you said "drop it." For the next few weeks at least, don't ask for a drop it without having started with a take it. Eventually, once you think your dog will drop just about any toy on cue, try asking her to drop a low value toy without having played the take it game first. If she does, jackpot her with great treats or especially exuberant play. When you think she's ready, try the same thing with an object she picked up that she shouldn't have—just be ready to instantly jackpot her with the canine equivalent of a free trip to Hawaii if she complies.

TUG OF WAR

Lots of dogs love to play tug of war, and you can use the game to entertain and exercise your dog. It has the additional benefit of helping your dog learn to handle emotional arousal, impulse control and how to be careful with his mouth. However, this is not a good game to play with dogs who have been aggressive around objects, or who become overly excited and can't calm them selves down. Overly excited dogs can switch from playful abandon to angry aggression as fast as sports fans, so don't play tug of war with a dog who can't control herself. You also want to be careful about letting young children play tug with a dog—we suggest keeping this as an "adult" game until you are sure your dog and child can play it together safely.

You might think, with all those cautions, that no one should play tug of war with their dog at all. It's true that for years, many trainers and behaviorists used to advise against it. However, if done correctly, tug of war can help to prevent the very problems described above. It can be a wonderful way to teach your dog to do what she's asked, even when excited.

Be careful about letting children play tug with a dog – we suggest keeping this as an "adult" game until you are sure your dog and child can play it together safely.

Start by putting some yummy treats in one hand, and then picking up a rope toy or a long plush toy that is suitable for tug games. The best toys are long enough to keep your dog's teeth at least a foot from your hand. Wave the end of the toy in front of your dog, and wait for her to take it in her mouth. Say "take it" if you've been working on take it/drop it in other contexts. Keep a hold of your end of the toy, and begin to pull back gently once she's gotten a good grip on the other end. Most dogs respond by pulling back themselves, and are more than happy to start playing tug with you. Pull backward a few times and have a short game of tug. (Be careful of tugging too hard from side to side, it can keep your dog's chiropractor busy if you do it too much.) Then, without releasing the toy, stop pulling, and bring that tasty treat in your other hand up to the dog's nose. As you do, say "drop it" just before she opens her mouth to take the treat.

Repeat that several times in a row, teaching her that it's in her best interest to give you the toy. The goal is to be able to play rousing games of tug, but still be able to stop the game immediately with a quiet word. Keep in mind that you need to be in control of this game—you're the one who should decide when to play and when to stop playing. You might be smart to keep the tug toy on the shelf until you want to play, so that you can initiate the game yourself.

YOU ARE NOT A DOG TOY

Playing with objects may be fun for your dog—but it won't be fun for you if you become one of the objects. Most dogs love to chase after moving things and grab at them with their mouths. Until they learn otherwise, those "things" can include your ankles and hands. After all, your dog began her life by playing with her littermates as her only toy—mouthing any body part she could get her jaws around, and wrestling with abandon with her brothers and sisters. It's your job to teach her how to play appropriately with you, and the first thing she needs to learn is that your body is off limits.

It may be natural for dogs to want to mouth your hand or nip at your ankles, but it can lead to trouble later in life. Dogs who learn to bite at body parts can inadvertently bite too hard or lose their tempers in an arousing play session. We can't expect a dog, an animal with far less

It's your job to teach her how to play appropriately with you, and the first thing she needs to learn is that your body is off limits.

cognitive ability than a human, to do any better than members of our own species at controlling emotional arousal. Humans are famous for turning games into fistfights or full-fledged riots, and we don't come equipped with carpet knives in our mouths. So, do your dog and your family a favor, and take the following to heart.

If your dog is still trying to play with your hands as if you were another puppy, do one of two things. You can help her learn to be gentle with her mouth by waiting for her to put a slight bit of pressure on your hand, and yelping as if you'd been shocked. Don't be shy about it—let a noise like "AWRP!" or "OUCH" bolt out of your mouth at a relatively loud volume. Your goal is to startle her, using the same sound she heard as a pup when she bit one of her littermates too hard. You are trying to teach her *bite inhibition*, and that the slightest pressure on your furless, pathetic little paws causes you pain and ends the play session.

The key to making this work long term is to immediately move your dog's attention to an appropriate toy. Be forewarned that the most common response of novices is to yelp, startle the dog as planned, and then stare back at the dog until she decides that the noise was a false alarm, that all is well, and so she leaps in again to bite at the closest body part. Avoid that by being ready to instantly redirect her attention to a toy after you yelp. It helps to be in the habit of having a toy always accessible. As soon as you redirect your dog to one toy, go find another one and tuck it away in your pocket, ready for the next time you need it.

WELL! I'M NOT GOING TO PLAY WITH *YOU* ANYMORE! Although the method above works beautifully on many dogs, it doesn't work with all of them. Some dogs respond to yelping by getting more excited and lunging in to bite harder, so experiment with this and base your subsequent response on her reaction. (Children, by the way, are rarely able to get dogs to stop mouthing by yelping themselves, but you can try yelping for them if your dog is getting too rough.) An alternative response to mouthing and nipping is to immediately end the play session. Stand up abruptly (I like to "huff" as if offended), and walk away, returning in one or two minutes to encourage object play again. If your dog attacks your ankles as you walk away (or any other time), get in the habit of tossing a small, harmless object to the ground to startle your dog (our favorite is a small, paperback book). Be sure

One alternative response to mouthing and nipping is to immediately end the play session.

that you don't hit your dog with it, but throw it between your dog and your ankles, hard enough to get a startle response. Don't say a word, just surprise your dog and then either leave the area for a minute or two, or redirect your dog to an appropriate toy. Don't worry if your dog proceeds to leap onto the object you threw down to startle him— you wanted him to stop biting at your ankles, and he did. Most dogs catch on after very few sessions. If you continue to have trouble you'd be wise to call in a coach (a dog trainer or behaviorist) who can help you teach your dog appropriate play behavior.

One last caveat about how *not* to play with your dog: please, please don't get down on the ground and wrestle play with your dog. That can be hard to say in dog training class, because some kind-hearted, dog-loving man's face always falls when the trainer says it. Make no mistake about it—with a few exceptions, this is a guy thing. Male primates engage in "rough and tumble" wrestle play so conspicuously that field researchers use it as an indicator of sex. Dogs love wrestling around on the floor, just as many people do, but wrestling teaches dogs to play rough with people, and it can lead to serious trouble. Perhaps not with the person who started it, but more likely with the little girl whose parents are suing you over the "play bite" to their daughter's face. Or to the younger, smaller family member who finds the dog constantly mouthing them and biting at their arm on leash walks. Instead, play ball, play Frisbee, play soccer, let your dog chase you (not vice versa), teach heel like a game, teach your dog to search for hidden toys, enroll in tracking or agility classes, do tricks together, herd sheep, go hunting, have a wonderful joyful time together, but please, please, *please* don't wrestle play with your dog.

TEACHING TRICKS TO FIDO THE WONDER DOG

Teaching tricks is another wonderful way to play with your dog. Trick training has the advantage of feeling silly and fun for both of you, while still teaching your dog that it's fun to pay attention. Tricks are also great mental exercise, and dogs need mental exercise as much as they need physical exercise. It makes sense if you think about it—our dogs' ancestors were problem-solving, strategic hunters who had to plan and coordinate their activities based on a complexity of factors. Many of our dogs are woefully under employed, and teaching tricks is a wonderful way to engage their brains. Learning new tricks seems to relax dogs as much as the same amount of physical exercise (and is more fun when it's fifteen below outside!).

The sky is the limit when training tricks, as long as you are aware of your dog's limitations and avoid situations in which he might hurt himself or be scared. You can use the same method you've been using throughout this book, rewarding successive approximations of what you want with tasty treats or play and praise, and end up teaching enough tricks to make your dog look like a movie star. We like to use clicker training when teaching tricks, because it allows you to give your dog feedback with such precision. Clicker training involves linking the sound of a click with a treat, so that you can click instantly when your dog does what you want. It's similar to verbal praise, but it's a sound that inherently gets your dog's attention and isn't used any other time. See the resource section at the back of the book for some books and videos that can get you started.

The tricks you can teach your dog are limited only by your dog's physical condition and your imagination. You can teach your dog to sit pretty (a good exercise for their hindquarters), to look sad (head flat on the ground between paws), to take a bow, spin, roll over, shake, pray, or even roll himself up in a blanket when you say "nighty-night." Aimee taught one of her dogs to run to the scale at the vet's office and sit and stay on it until they can record his weight. My dogs roll onto their sides and their backs when asked, all the better for examinations by vets. Both of those "tricks" are good reminders that there's a practical side of trick training—you can use them to make visits to the veterinarian more fun for everyone. There are lots more tricks you can teach your dog, including teaching a dog to "target" toward any object so that you can move him around in space, just like a dog in the movies. If you're lucky, you can find a training center that offers trick classes, which can be tremendous fun for both you and your dog. We teach tricks in our classes and you can't tell who is having more fun—the dogs, the owners or the trainers. Try it yourself—you'll be glad you did.

IT'S ALL A TRICK WHEN YOU GET DOWN TO IT There's no reason not to think of sit and lie down as tricks too, and that might be a good thing. People seem to be more relaxed and cheerful when they are teaching their dogs "tricks," rather than what has traditionally been called "obedience." They also often have more realistic expectations about tricks, rather than expecting their dogs to obey out of respect and submission. This week, try thinking of all the things you ask your dog to do as circus tricks that you've taught him for your own amusement. Remember too what was said earlier: you get back what you put in. If you want your dog to be enthusiastic, then be sure to be enthusiastic yourself. Of course, every dog is different, and it's true that some dogs are naturally reserved. However, time after time trainers see dogs plodding through an exercise until the trainer takes over with sparkling eyes and an exuberant voice. Within seconds it looks like she's working with a different dog, who is now joyfully charging through the exercises. Keep this in mind when you practice the exercises below . . .

THIS WEEK'S EXERCISES

SIT AND DOWN

At this point, most dogs will be ready for you to discontinue special training sessions for sitting on cue. Rather than asking for several sits in a row, get in the habit of asking for a sit just once, scattered throughout the day, as part of your dog's normal routine. This is a great exercise to think of as a trick—you want your dog to learn that sitting on cue is fun, no matter when or where it's performed. Ask your dog to sit as if it was the coolest thing in the world, using your voice to convey playful exuberance. When your dog sits, cheer, clap and dash off to the closest toy and throw it for him. Your goal this week is to ask for a sit in a range of locations and contexts so that he sits wherever and whenever asked.

Dogs will vary in how they are doing with down. Some dogs won't be ready yet to lie down at a moment's notice without a bit of visual prompting. That's okay, but continue decreasing the movements of your arm to get your dog's head directed toward the ground. Try standing up straight, shoulders back, and asking your dog to down without any movement at all. If he lies down to the verbal cue alone, give him a jackpot to make him happy that he was so clever. However, some dogs at this stage will still need at least a small arm motion from

Try standing up straight, shoulders back, and asking your dog to down without any movement at all. If he lies down to the verbal cue alone, give him a jackpot.

you. Try to sweep your hand downward without moving your torso forward, and experiment with how little you can move your arm and still get him to lie down. Remember your goal of teaching him to sit or lie down in response to either a verbal or a visual signal. You can always go back to using them together if he needs a bit of convincing, but it's handy to have a dog who will respond to both your voice and your hand signals.

THE NAME GAME

Take a few minutes to review the level of distraction you've been asking your dog to turn away from, and ask yourself how successful you and your dog have been.

Scatter some sessions of the name game throughout the week, being sure to distinguish between it and the attention game. Recall that the attention game teaches dogs to check in with their humans when they're in distracting environments. The name game teaches your dog that she should give you her full attention if she hears her name. Since this will be the fifth week you've worked on the name game, it's time to consciously focus on two things: 1) increasing the level of distraction with which you're competing, and 2) varying what happens when your dog looks at you when you say her name. This is a great time to intersperse using play and treats as reinforcements, teaching your dog the benefits of giving you her attention.

INCREASING THE LEVEL OF DISTRACTON It's always tricky for dog trainers to provide a formula about exactly how to accomplish working through distractions, because at this stage, each step in training depends on how the dog did on the step before. Additionally, as we all know, dogs differ in what distracts them and how distracted they can be by events in the environment. What's consistently true is that we need to be aware of how distracting any one event is to each individual dog, and how the dog is doing at each level of difficulty.

Take a few minutes to review the level of distraction you've been asking your dog to turn away from, and ask yourself how successful you and your dog have been. If your dog has been doing well, then up the distraction level from a maximum of 4 or 5 to a level 6 or 7. If things aren't going well, then you're probably pushing things too far too fast. Don't worry when you get an occasional failure—it's not a problem if a six-month old Gordon Setter stays riveted on a pheasant in a corn field, or an adolescent Border Collie can't take her eye off her first herd of sheep. Simply record those events as "distraction level 10's" in your mind, be thankful for a good collar or harness system, and go back to working at a level at which you both can succeed.

VARYING THE REINFORCEMENT Use your best and tastiest treats for the higher-level distractions, but start varying the reinforcement for turning toward you when things are a bit easier for your dog. If Ginger's head whips around when you say her name during a quiet spell in the backyard, hold off on the treat and do something else that she thinks is fun. You could turn and run away from her and let her chase you, or surprise her by throwing her favorite toy. Try cooing "good girl," rubbing her chest in just the way she loves, then saying "okay" and letting her go off and do her own thing for awhile. Alternatively, you could get her leash and take her on a quick walk, or jingle your car keys and go for a short ride.

LEAVE IT

This week you're going to ask your dog to leave something alone that is not in your hand, but is on the ground behind you. This step is a LOT harder for your dog, so don't toss a treat on the ground, say "leave it" and expect your dog to back away. She's been scarfing up goodies from the ground ever since she could walk, and she's not going to translate "leave it" from food *in your hand* to food *on the ground* without your help. Getting this to work (and it does!) depends on your attention to detail, so read the following carefully before you proceed.

Begin as you did last week with a low-value treat in one hand and a high-value treat in the other. Repeat the exercise as described last week, by showing your dog the low-value treat, saying "leave it" and giving her the extra good food from the other hand if she responds correctly. Once that has gone well two times in a row, stand up and face your dog, and show her another low-value treat. Say "leave it," but this time toss it a few feet behind you. Be sure that you give the verbal cue *before* you throw the treat; that's one of the details that's especially important. It's much harder for a dog to stop going forward once they're halfway there, so give her a chance to be right, and say "leave it" clearly and firmly before she's motivated to dash to the treat.

She's been scarfing up goodies from the ground ever since she could walk, and she's not going to translate "leave it" from food in your hand to food on the ground without your help.

In an ideal world, the treat will have fallen two to three feet behind you and about a foot to the side. That location is best because it gives you the ability to body block her if she goes for the treat as soon as it hits the ground. Most dogs will do exactly that, charging for it as soon as the treat hits the ground, so be ready to move quickly between her and the treat. Some dogs will immediately defer to your body block, looking up at your face and even backing up a foot or two. If so, thank your lucky stars that you have such a wonderful dog, say "Good!" and give her the food in your hand. Most dogs, however, have no intention of giving up that fast, so they counter your movement by trying to go around you. Your job is to keep your dog from getting the treat, so act like a goalie at a soccer game. Move left or right, doing whatever you need to do to block her from getting the treat, just as you'd try to block a ball from going into the net. Meanwhile, watch for the slightest sign that your dog is hesitating, and is no longer trying to get the treat on the ground. Obvious signs of that are looking up at your face, backing up an inch or two, or walking away as if bored. However, some dogs will merely shift their bodies backward the slightest bit. That's fine—you want to reinforce your dog for any action that tells you she's stopped trying to get at the treat, even if just for a moment.

If you have a relentless dog who never gives up, or is so fast that you can't block her, try stepping lightly on the treat, so that your dog can't possibly get at it. Wait her out—eventually she'll move her head in another direction, and you can instantly praise and then treat her. Distract her from the treat on the floor with a treat in your hand, and then pick the low-value treat up off the floor.

Practice this throughout the week, tossing the treat on the ground from different hands, in different locations, but remember to only throw treats that aren't going to send your dog into a frenzy. You can work up to bigger challenges later, but right now you're busy building a strong foundation. You can also use objects rather than food, perhaps a toy that your dog likes but isn't crazy-in-love with. Don't push this further than your dog is prepared to go—for example, resist the urge to use it when your dog starts to pick up the remote control. (Although, if you can't contain yourself and you find yourself blurting it out when you shouldn't have, be ready to jackpot your dog if by some miracle she listens and backs away!) You'll need several more weeks or months of practice before you can use this when your dog is several feet in front of you and comes upon a soggy bag of french fries. [18]

STAY

Continue increasing the distance, duration or the level of distractions while your dog is on a sit/stay, being careful to work on only one of the "D's" at a time. Try for a few short sessions a day, remembering to make staying in place the fun part for your dog and to make the release the boring part. Keep your voice quiet so that you don't get him so excited he can't hold his stay. If things are going well, this is a good week to ask your dog to stay while lying down. A down stay is a wonderful trick to have in your repertoire. It has a multitude of benefits, including teaching impulse control to your dog, and allowing you to have a quiet dinner without feeling like a jackal is drooling over your shoulder. A down/stay is also an excellent way to keep a group of dogs from getting overly aroused—many professional trainers ask their dogs to do a half hour down/stay every evening, and there's no reason you can't too. Down/stays are especially useful when you want your dog to stay in place longer than a few seconds. Many dogs aren't comfortable sitting on their haunches for very long, and tend to want to lie down when put on sit/stay for any length of time. You can prevent this by using down/stay any time you want your dog to settle into a stay for more than a few seconds.

Start in a quiet room when your dog is relatively relaxed and ask him to sit and then lie down. Pay attention to his posture once he is down. Dogs can be lying down flat on their bellies with all four legs tucked underneath them—the better to spring up at a moment's notice, or they can be lying down with their hips flipped over to one side. The latter is what you want, because it makes your dog more likely to stay in place once asked. If your dog doesn't flip his hips by himself, you can encourage him to do so by luring his nose back toward his shoulder with a treat. This helps to cause his hips to flip over onto their side. Once he's in that position, use your praise word to reinforce it, and then quickly say "stay" and hold your hand out like a traffic cop.

Be sure to use the same verbal and visual signal you've been using to

A down stay has a multitude of benefits, including teaching impulse control to your dog, and allowing you to have a quiet dinner without feeling like a jackal is drooling over your shoulder.

---

[18] Don't do this exercise by yourself if your dog has ever been aggressive around food. If that's been a problem, don't hesitate to call in a professional and follow their advice about how to proceed.

WEEK FIVE

Keep your praise and your own body movements quiet and calm, otherwise you can hype your dog up so that she can't sit down even if she wanted to.

ask him to stay when he was sitting—this is no time for variations on your signals. Remember to avoid saying "stay" as if it were a question—a rising inflection might encourage your dog to get up and be active. You don't need to belt it out, but you want to say "stay" as if it were a statement, not a question. Additionally, pay attention to where you are in space: you'll have the best luck if you're about one to two feet away from your dog—if you're too close he'll feel like you are looming over him and want to break his stay to move away.

Use the same routine you've used for sit/stays. After asking for the stay, rock forward and, with an underhanded motion, sweep a treat into his mouth. Be ready to body block if you see any sign that he's about to get up, but don't loom over him too closely—give him some room to breathe. After a brief second or two, say "okay" and walk away. Remind yourself that the release should be downright boring—now is not the time to pet or praise him. Once he's up, walk a few feet away and ask for a down again. Repeat the entire exercise four or five times, ending on a good note if at all possible. Try for two or three sessions a day if you can manage them.

FOUR ON THE FLOOR

This week your dog is going to take one step closer to that automatic sit you've been working towards. Remember that last week you asked your dog to sit a couple of times in a row when a visitor came, and then waited for her to sit automatically the third time the visitor approached. This time you should give her a chance to sit automatically the *first* time anyone approaches or enters the house. If she does, she should hear lots of praise and get a jackpot of yummy treats. If she doesn't, don't worry, just have the person turn away and try again, this time asking for the sit. Repeat this a few times, and then give your dog another chance to sit on her own. Be forewarned, at this stage of training some dogs will be shining stars at the automatic sit, and others will be, uhhhh . . . a bit slower to catch on. Lassie (my Lassie, the one who came when called without any training) didn't stop leaping onto visitor's shoulders for months after I got her, so don't despair if you have a jumper. Time heals all—even scratch wounds on your chest from exuberant leapers.

One word of caution: Be sure that your own actions aren't working against you. Keep your praise and your own body movements quiet and calm, otherwise you can hype your dog up so that she can't sit down even if she wanted to. Get in the habit of using praise words quietly, using long, slow sounds rather than short, choppy ones. This is especially important for those extra exuberant dogs who explode in excitement with the slightest encouragement.

HEEL

THE FOLLOW GAME CONTINUES Continue to reinforce your dog for finding heel position, but this week use your leash and walk in a random pattern. After all, you can't always walk in a circle in the neighborhood, and you both need to get used to walking together with a leash between you. Walk ten strides in one direction and fifteen in another to get him used to staying with you wherever you go. Remember, it's his job to catch up to you—try to avoid prompting him with claps and smooches, letting him make his own decisions. Continue to stay quiet—next week you'll begin saying "heel," but until you can elicit a behavior that looks like heel there's no point in using the word as a cue. Treat your dog whenever he's beside you, but this week keep walking as you treat, rather than stopping first. If necessary, use the treat as a lure to keep him at your side once he joins up with you.

If your dog ignores you and walks to the end of the leash, simply stop and wait for him to look or move toward you. Praise him the moment that he does, even if all he does is turn his head. Once he moves into heel position, shower him with treats and move forward energetically to keep his attention. Continue to give him lots of reinforcement if he keeps up with you. Remember—heeling isn't natural to dogs, and it goes against their instincts. Your job is to be the most interesting thing around, and you've got a lot of competition out there.

Guard against "fixing" things by going back to your dog so that he is in heel position because of your actions. This is a natural thing to do, but it's not going to teach your dog to attend to you. Rather, it will teach your dog that he can count on you to fix things and get yourself back into heel position. Good human!

Keep these sessions short and upbeat, sprinkling one or two of them

Treat your dog whenever he's beside you, but this week keep walking as you treat, rather than stopping first.

throughout the day as you do your other exercises. You might even try starting your neighborhood leash walks out with a few strides of heeling, then releasing your dog quickly so that he can sniff and relax on the walk. It's too much work for dogs to concentrate on the heel exercise throughout the entire walk, especially in the early stages of training, so release him right away with a clear signal. Let a well-fitted harness or head halter keep him from pulling you down the sidewalk like a draft horse for the rest of the walk. Some dogs will do better if you practice heel at the end of the walk, being a bit less wild-eyed than when they started out. Do whatever works best for you, but try to get in at least one short heel session every day.

COME, ATTENTION GAME, WAIT

Continue working on these exercisess when you can, using the same methods and expectations from last week. Try to incorporate them into play as often as you can, so that your dog can't tell the difference between "obedience" and "tricks."

Note to dedicated dog owners: if you're feeling a bit overwhelmed right around now, take heart. All these exercises are actually harder to read about than to do, as long as you get in the habit of scattering exercises throughout the day. Don't worry if you have a busy day and can only include a few of the exercises during one particular day. We're describing an ideal schedule of training, but most of us with day jobs can't practice every single exercise as often as we'd like. That's okay—hopefully you'll have your dog a long, long time and have plenty of opportunities to build on your successes. We'll talk more in the next chapter about how to integrate dog training into the rest of your life, so that it gets easier and easier every week.

WEEKLY SUMMARY

• PLAY Concentrate on teaching your dog appropriate ways to play with objects, and on inhibiting your dog from playing with you as if you were a toy. Teach "take it/drop it" as a game, and play tug of war IF you control the object and you use it to teach your dog emotional control, rather than as a way to overly arouse him. Try thinking of all the exercises you've been working on as tricks that will keep you and your dog light-hearted.

• SIT AND DOWN Start asking for sits just once, scattered throughout the day as part of your dog's daily routine. Keep working on using only one cue with sit, staying still when you say "sit," and remaining silent when you use your visual signal. (But go back to using both if your dog is overwhelmed with distractions.) Work on "disappearing" the visual cue for lie down, saying "down" first and then using the smallest movement with your arm that you can manage.

• NAME GAME Begin to increase the level of distraction, assuming that your dog has been doing well at easier levels. Spend some time thinking about what level of distraction your dog can handle. If your dog is doing well at easier levels, it's time to increase the level of distraction a notch or two. It's also time to start varying the type of reinforcement your dog gets for giving you her attention.

• LEAVE IT This week you're going to ask your dog to "leave it" when the object of interest is on the ground. Start by reviewing last week's exercise, asking your dog to ignore food in your hand. The third time, say "leave it" and toss the low-value treat behind, and slightly to the side. The instant your dog stops trying to get to the food on the ground, praise and give her the better food from your other hand.

• STAY For sit/stay, continue as before, but increase the difficulty level of ONE of the three "D's—distance, duration or distraction—at a time. This week add in down/stay, being sure that your dog is lying down with his hips flipped to the side in a relaxed position before you say "stay."

• FOUR ON THE FLOOR Give your dog a chance to sit automatically the first time she sees a visitor approaching. Give her a jackpot if she sits on her own without any prompting from you (but don't undermine your efforts by overly exciting her with your voice). If she doesn't sit on her own, have the visitor ask her to sit several times in a row, and then give her another chance to do it herself.

• HEEL This week walk purposefully with your dog on leash in a random pattern, waiting for your dog to choose to link up with you like you did last week. Treat your dog whenever he's beside you, but this week keep walking as you treat, rather than stopping first. If your dog ignores you and gets to the end of the leash, stop and wait for him to attend to you. When he does, even if it's just a turn of the head, praise and treat, and stride off enthusiastically to keep his attention on you.

• COME, WAIT and the ATTENTION GAME Scatter these throughout the week as well, thinking of them as tricks as much as anything else. You can make practicing come, wait and the attention game as fun as any sport if you are enthusiastic and playful. Before you know it, you're dog will be begging to practice being obedient.

A DAY IN THE LIFE

ARE WE THERE YET? We've covered a lot in this little book, and you well might be wondering when you're going to be "done" training your dog. When can you step back a bit and relax? After all, you've been working on a lot of material: teaching your dog to pay attention, to respond to his name, to come, sit, down, stay, wait, leave it and heel when asked. Wow, that's a lot—and not just for your dog. You are learning the signals as well, working on being consistent and clear, and continually evaluating where you are now and how best to proceed. The good news is, that although you'll always be training your dog to some extent, it gets a lot easier in the weeks and months to come. Once you've created a solid foundation, you can decrease the number of "training sessions" and incorporate the exercises into your dog's daily routine.

INTEGRATE TRAINING INTO YOUR DAY Once you get in the habit, it's easy to integrate training into your day. Our dogs always want something, whether it's to go on a walk or to get a belly rub, so you can ask your dog to listen to you as a way of getting what he wants. The following is an example of training combined with everyday living. Of course, the specifics will vary from dog to dog, but this example shows how seamlessly you can incorporate training into your daily routine.

Imagine you've just gotten up and it's time to let Jack, your eight-month old Miniature Schnauzer, out to potty:

~ Pick up some small tasty treats as you walk over to Jack in his crate or pen.

Once you get in the habit, it's easy to integrate training into your day.

~ Open the crate and ask for an immediate sit. Praise as soon as he does, and walk with him to the door.

~ Ask Jack to "wait" and open the door. Release as soon as he politely hesitates, and go outside with him.

~ After he's had a minute to sniff around, turn away from him and say "Jack, come!" in an enthusiastic voice. Run away from him, clapping your hands as you go. The instant that he turns and begins to run toward you, praise him with "Good!" and either give him a treat or run in another direction and let him chase you some more. Repeat this two or three more times.

~ Pick up his favorite outdoor toy and say "take it" as you hand it to him. Let him run and play with it, or play tug with him for a while. If necessary, move a treat to his nose and say "drop," pick up the toy and give him the treat.

~ Take your attention off Jack, and walk together around the yard, letting him relax and sniff around.

~ When you return to the house, say "wait" before you open the door. Release him with a clear signal and let him bound into the house.

All of the above could easily occur in less than five minutes. In that short period of time you practiced come, sit, wait, take it, and drop. That's five exercises in only a few minutes. Not only does this kind of training schedule make it easier on you, it also means that your dog is more likely to listen when you need him to. Dogs often seem to understand the difference between a formal "training session" and "real life," and if you want them to listen all of the time, it's important to practice throughout the day.

HOW GOOD IS GOOD ENOUGH?

The question that began this chapter—"how long does this take?"—can't be answered unless you know what you'll expect from your dog once she's grown up. How reliable do you want your dog to be? Do you want a dog who comes ninety percent of the time out of a fenced back yard, or an off-leash dog who always comes when called even after flushing a deer in the woods? The former is the equivalent of eighth grade math, while the latter assumes a level of mathematical mastery you'd expect from a Ph.D. As we all know, different levels of skill take different amounts of time and energy. That's as true in dog training as it is in anything else. This may seem obvious, but many people make the mistake of investing enough time and energy to train their dogs at an eighth grade level, and yet expect them to perform as if they have completed graduate school.

At the same time, most of us have other things to do besides training our dogs. The solution is to work on mastering one or two exercises at a time, while continuing to let the "day in the life" scenario maintain the rest of our training. Ask yourself what signals are the most important ones for your household—what do you most want your dog to be able to do when things get a bit chaotic? Everyone is different, but many people would be thrilled to have a dog who comes when called, walks beside them politely on leash and doesn't jump up. If you think about it, mastery of those three simple exercises means you can take your dog just about anywhere, anytime, and have the experience be fun for both of you. Of course, calling them "simple" doesn't mean that you can expect your dog to have mastered them in a few weeks or months. Some dogs will require months or even years of training to be reliable, and truth be told, some can never be trusted to come when called when off leash. However, focusing special attention on "key" exercises will go a long way toward having the dog of your dreams.

STEP BY STEP The trick to mastering an exercise is to understand the importance of gradually increasing its difficulty—neither asking too much nor too little of your dog at any given time. Here's an example of how to do that using the exercise "leave it." Last week you asked your dog to "leave it" when you placed a low-value treat behind you and ever so slightly to the side. This week you'll practice the exercise by taking a bigger step to the side, leaving a clear path between your dog and the treat.

Let's say your dog is doing great. By the end of week six you can say "leave it," drop food behind and slightly to the side of you, and expect your dog to leave it alone. But ask yourself: would that work when you're on a walk in the neighborhood and Ginger, who is ten feet in front of you, spots a half-eaten candy bar on the sidewalk? If you say

The trick to mastering an exercise is to understand the importance of gradually increasing its difficulty.

"leave it" what do you think will happen? Your dog might stop and stand still while you pick up the candy bar and place it in the garbage, but then, the moon might be made of asiago cheese and pigs might fly. It's possible that you are lucky enough to have a dog like that, but if you do, you probably don't need this book. The vast majority of dogs, perhaps 995 out of 1,000 of them, aren't going to relate "leave it" in a carefully controlled training session with "leave it" when they're cruising along in front of you on a regular walk and they serendipitously come upon a treasure.

What are the differences between the two scenarios above? First, think about how far away the food is in your practice sessions versus the example above. You'll need to gradually increase the distance between you and your dog, not jump from two feet to ten feet with no steps in between. Also, notice that the food is behind you in the training exercise, but the food is in front of both you and your dog on the walk. That's an extremely important difference to your dog. Additionally, you've been working on leave it as part of a training session. That's appropriate at this stage of training--you're laying a foundation under the right circumstances so that you and your dog can be successful. There are no major distractions, you have your dog's attention and the dog is set up to do it right and be reinforced. However, to get this to work in real life you need to gradually increase the difficulty level by 1) increasing the distance between you and the object, 2) changing your location relative to the food such that it is at first behind and to the side of you, then beside you and eventually in front of both of you and your dog, 3) practicing in a variety of contexts, including on leash walks when your dog doesn't expect it and 4) changing what you drop so that your dog generalizes it to all objects.

Don't expect your dog to master this exercise in a few weeks, or even months. It's reasonable to expect some dogs to take a year to master this exercise so that they will ignore virtually anything if asked. (Take heart, that doesn't mean it won't work most of the time.) If a year sounds like a long time, think about what you're asking of your dog: ignore something amazingly wonderful that's right in front of his face because you asked him. How many people would do that?!

PRACTICE REALLY DOES MAKE PERFECT (OR CLOSE ENOUGH)!

Students in dog training classes often ask: "Are we going to learn anything new next week? If not, I might skip class because it's such a busy week for us." Given how busy we all are, it's a reasonable question. However, the value of class isn't only in learning new exercises, it's in the opportunity to practice in a supportive environment, with a coach at your side, in an environment with built-in distractions. Dogs are no different than human students in many ways—they need to be introduced to new material in a supportive environment, and then have lots of opportunities to practice their skills in a variety of contexts. That's why our kids go to soccer and ballet practice. No matter how talented, people still need coaches to tell them how they are doing and to help them improve. After all, even Tiger Woods has a coach. Training involves rewiring the brains and bodies of both you and your dog, and that isn't going happen if you don't get in a lot of practice.

The need for practice is one of the reasons that play is so useful in training. It's much easier to think about playing a game with your dog than it is to think about the need for frequent "training sessions." Everyone is better at cards or video games if they practice—but we don't call it "practice," we call it playing a game. As long as you're using positive reinforcement, your dog will think of practice as a game too, and enjoy every minute of it. People don't get tired of "practicing" their serve if they love playing tennis, and they don't get bored counting cards if they love to play bridge. Don't worry that this won't feel "serious" enough: games have rules too, that's why they're called games.

TRAINING EQUALS BONDING The other advantage to playing/practicing with your dog on a daily basis is that it creates a structure in which you can interact with your dog. Dogs are highly social animals; if they weren't, we wouldn't all get along so well. However, it's so easy on a busy day to open the door to a fenced yard when we get home, assuming that our dogs will go outside and amuse themselves. Some dogs do, but most want you to come out and play with them. (That's why they ask to go out, and then ask immediately to come in again—they may want to be outside, but not without you.) Dogs want to do things with you, and they don't think training is

Training involves rewiring both you and your dog's brain, and that won't happen if your don't get in a lot of practice.

work, they think it's fun. Why wouldn't they? They get to be with you, they get mental and physical exercise, and they get treats and play and belly rubs.

THIS WEEK'S EXERCISES

THE NAME GAME

You probably don't need to spend much time on this exercise at this point, but don't forget to practice in situations that are highly distracting for your dog. Try it on walks when your dog sees another dog across the street, in the house after your dog has greeted visitors, or in the lobby of the vet clinic. Be sure to jackpot any remarkable responses (a terrier turning away from a newly discovered rabbit den deserves the doggy equivalent of Filet Mignon with Rosemary Reduction Sauce).

LEAVE IT

As mentioned earlier, this week you'll want to toss the treat a bit further away than last week. There should be a clear path between your dog and the treat, which makes it a little bit more difficult—and a little bit more like real life. However, it won't be too hard, because you'll still be close enough to the path between the treat and your dog to be able to block her if she goes for the food after you say "leave it." Try to be a few feet away from your dog—if you're too close it's actually harder to block her than if there's a bit of room between the two of you. Say "leave it" before you toss the treat—remember that saying "leave it' before she sees the food makes it easier for her to comply. At this stage, it's too much to expect her to stop if you say "leave it" after she's already started going for the food.

If your dog is doing well, it's time to help your dog to generalize the exercise. You can do that by practicing in different locations, tossing the food with your other hand or placing it on the ground, and using toys instead of food. If it's not going smoothly yet, don't worry. It takes some dogs a lot longer to master this, but that doesn't mean they won't be good at it eventually.

FOUR ON THE FLOOR

Continue working on the "automatic sit," in which an approaching visitor becomes the cue for your dog to sit. You'll do best if you vary your expectations depending on the level of difficulty. Give your dog a chance to sit automatically as the visitor approaches IF you're working on this when your dog is relatively mellow, and you're in a context in which she's likely to succeed. However, if she's just bounded out of her crate and there's a party going on outside your front door, help her out by asking for the sit before she has a chance to forget her manners and jump up.

HEEL

PUTTING HEEL ON CUE Once your dog is readily "finding the heel position" and staying with you for several paces at a time, introduce the cue "heel." Ask your dog to sit, and prime him with a treat when he does. Say "heel!" in an energetic voice, and stride forward. If he moves forward with you, say your praise word and treat him after only one or two strides of walking side by side. Don't be stingy—it's better to err on the side of giving too many treats at this point rather than too few. If you need to, let the treat act as a lure to keep him at your side as you walk, but work on raising your arm whenever you can so that he doesn't become dependent on seeing your hand in front of him as a cue. Gradually increase the time period between treats, asking your dog to stay up with you for three strides, then five, etc. etc. After a minute or two of successful training, release your dog with the same cue you use for wait and stay and let him relax.

Heel is like a circus trick that takes lots of attention, so don't ask for it casually and expect your dog to heel beside you for a twenty-minute walk.

Remember that heel is like a circus trick that takes lots of attention, so don't ask for it casually and expect your dog to heel beside you for a twenty-minute walk. A few dogs will walk shoulder to shoulder with you with little training, but most of them find it difficult, so interweave short sessions of heeling into long, casual walks. Use a harness or head collar to keep your dog from pulling on long walks, and you'll soon find that your dog gets better and better at heeling when you ask him for it.

You can use heel when you need your dog close to you for the sake of safety—walking into a vet clinic, crossing busy streets even if on leash, or when you spot a dog in the neighborhood who doesn't look very friendly. It's a handy signal to have, and a wonderful way to improve your training skills, so keep practicing it when you have time.

STAY

This week, ask your dog to stay for longer periods of time, and to wait longer between treats. As always, start where she can win, in an environment without a lot of distractions, and when she's not bouncing off the walls. Ask her to sit or lie down, give her a clear visual and verbal signal for stay and back up one or two feet. If you've been returning every few seconds, start expecting her to wait longer between treats. There's no magic formula that says exactly how long you should wait, because some high-energy dogs will still need three or four treats in a six second period, while others will only need one. Try to arrange it so that your dog is succeeding eighty percent of the time. If her success rate is much less, you need to make the exercise a bit easier by asking for shorter stays or being closer to your dog. If it is higher, you're not pushing the envelope, so your dog is probably ready to stay a bit longer or with fewer treats.

Remember to work on duration and distance separately, and ask for the briefest of stays when you increase the distance you move away from your dog.

Remember that you're an active participant in this training. Be primed and ready for your dog to break, and to move as necessary to block any breaks by "taking the space" yourself. Do be sure to take the pressure off and back up yourself the instant that your dog hesitates by stopping or rocking backward.

WORK ON DISTANCE SEPARATELY In a separate session, begin to ask your dog to stay when you are farther away. Remember to work on duration and distance separately, so ask for the briefest of stays when you increase the distance you move away from your dog. How far you go depends, of course, on your dog. Some dogs will do fine if you back up four or five feet away from them, as long as you return right away to give them a treat while they are holding their stay. Others need to be nursed, one step at a time, from one foot to two feet to three feet … Base your decisions on your dog's abilities, pushing the envelope only if you have achieved at least eighty percent success at a particular distance. Remember too, that distractions are what make stays most difficult for dogs, so always be aware of the level of distraction under which you're working, and manage distance and duration accordingly.

COME

LESS IS MORE Perhaps the hardest part of teaching a reliable recall is learning when not to call your dog to come. Novice dog trainers call their dogs to come when there's no chance of the dog complying, and they repeat "Fido COME!" four times in a row when it clearly isn't going to work. Prevent that by pausing before you call your dog, and asking yourself what the probability is that your dog will respond correctly. If you wouldn't bet five bucks that he'll come when called, resist calling and go closer to him. Being closer might be all that's needed if he's only moderately distracted. If he's completely absorbed in something, you might need to go all the way to him, wave a treat in front of his nose, and then call him to come to you after you back up a step.

Work also on training yourself to call "come!" once, and then either reinforce a good response or, if he doesn't respond correctly, to go closer to him and get his attention. It takes a lot of training to keep from repeating yourself—it seems to be hard-wired into us to say "come" again and again, usually louder and louder, in hopes of getting what we want.[19] So cover your mouth with your hand (don't laugh, I actually had to do that one summer to stop from repeating "lie down" to my herding dog), bite your tongue or use duct tape, but try as hard as you can to avoid repeating the word "come" when you call your dog.

HIDE AND SEEK Here's a fun game to play when you're working on come training: Wait for your dog to be distracted by something, and then hide behind a door or a tree in the backyard. Call him to come, clap your hands a few times, and then go still. Peek just enough to see what your dog is doing. If he's completely ignoring you, get closer to him and call again, or play the game another day. If, on the other hand, he hears you and starts looking for you, he most likely won't be sure exactly where you are. That makes you all the more interesting, and puts you into that compelling "hard to get" category. Give him a few seconds to try to find you, but if he can't figure out where you are, clap and call again before your dog gets too panicked about having lost you. Most dogs seem to be thrilled when they solve the puzzle, so have a party when you meet up, and plan to play again sometime soon.

---

[19] Who was it who defined insanity as doing the same thing over and over again, and expecting a different response?

You can play a great variant of this game in which you clap to get your dog's attention, call come and then dash away and pretend to hide behind a tree or bush. In this case your dog will know exactly where you are, but it still all feels like a great game. You can squeal when your dog "finds" you, dash away to "hide" again, play tag around a tree or bush and then stop and have a good giggle together.

WAIT

Your job is to remember to say "wait" before you open the door, and to be conscious of all the cues that your dog thinks are relevant to your expectations.

This week you're going to increase the practicality of the exercise by changing your position relative to your dog. So far, you've been walking to the door with your dog, both facing the same way, and then turning to face your dog so that you're between her and the door. That face-to-face contact helps your dog hesitate after you say wait, but you're not going to want to go through life turning the opposite way from which you want to go. Thus, the next step is to say "wait" while you and your dog are both facing toward the door. Many dogs will stop when they hear the cue and pause until they hear your release word. If that describes your dog, instantly release and have a party outside for your wonderful, special dog. Many other perfectly lovely dogs will ignore the word "wait," and plow forward as if you hadn't said anything at all. That's an understandable response: previously they were using context as a cue as well as the sound of your voice, and now you've changed things around. If that happens, respond by moving between your dog and the door, turning back toward her and backing her up with a gentle body block. Resist repeating the cue; stay silent while you are backing you're dog up. Move yourself back to the door, and be ready to open it if your dog stays in place momentarily. Release her as soon as she hesitates, and then repeat the exercise with your body turned part way toward the door. Gradually work up to asking for a wait when your dog is in front of you and facing the same direction.

Wait is a perfect exercise to integrate into your dog's daily life. Every dog has to go out several times a day, so your "practice sessions" are already scheduled for you. Your job is to remember to say "wait" before you open the door, and to be conscious of all the things—such as the way you are facing—that might be meaningful to your dog.

WEEKLY SUMMARY

- **THE ROAD TO PERFECTION** Decide as a family which behaviors are most important for your dog to master, and think through a step-by-step plan to get from where you are now to where you want to go. Meanwhile, integrate all your exercises into your dog's day as much as you can, so that the line between "training" and "living" becomes fuzzy.

- **NAME GAME** Remember to take treats or toys with you when out on walks or excursions, and be ready to treat your dog when you say his name. Start asking for his attention at moderate to higher levels of distraction this week, making mental notes about what he can handle and which distractions are still too much for him.

- **LEAVE IT** This week you'll say "leave it" first, and then toss the treat a few feet behind you, but also a bit more to the side than last week. Your dog should have a clear path to the treat this time, which you'll block with your legs if she decides to try for it. Remember to reinforce any hesitation with food from the other hand, and jackpot any particularly stellar performances.

- **HEEL** Work with your dog on leash this week, but continue to wait for your dog to attend to you, rather than vice versa. Ask your dog to sit, give him a treat and then begin to walk in a random pattern. Praise and treat every time he is in heel position, and if it's going well, continue walking forward while you treat. Some dogs will be ready to walk for ten or twenty yards at your side, while others will only manage a few paces. If your dog lags behind you, stop before the leash tugs him, and wait for him to look at you. Praise as soon as he does, and treat liberally when he gets himself back in heel position. If you need to, use a treat in your hand to keep him at your side once he's joined up with you. Gradually, over time, ask him to walk beside you for longer periods without a treat as a lure, saying "heel" as you start out and "okay" to release him.

- **STAY** Start to ask for stays that last longer, perhaps ten to twenty seconds, depending on how your dog is doing. Continue to treat as he's staying in place, but if he's doing well, increase the time between treats. Always be ready to body block if your dog start to break the stay, but remember to take the pressure off him the instant that he rocks backward and settles back down. In separate sessions, increase the distance between you and your dog, being sure to keep the duration very short. As always, be aware of the level of distraction, and only ask for short, easy stays if your dog is surrounded by especially interesting events.

• COME Continue making coming when called a fun game for your dog, adding "hide and seek" to your list of games. Concentrate this week on saying "come" only once, and not repeating yourself if it doesn't work. Practice the habit of going closer to your dog, getting his attention and then calling again, rather than standing still and calling repeatedly.

• WAIT Work towards making this exercise practical by saying "wait" while both you and your dog are facing the door. Open the door and release immediately if your dog responds correctly, and go back to body blocking your dog away from the door if she forged ahead of you.

• ATTENTION, FOUR ON THE FLOOR, SIT AND DOWN Integrate these exercises into your day, ensuring that your dog learns that his behavior leads to what he wants. A correct response to "sit" gets him a belly rub or his dinner. A look in your direction gets a toy tossed or a treat popped into his mouth. For all we know, he probably thinks he's training you—but who cares, as long as he does what he is asked and you are both happy?

"KNOWING" ISN'T EVERYTHING

Here's one last question for you before you close the covers on this book. What would you say if someone asked "Does your dog know how to sit when asked?" If you asked a hundred dog owners this question, most of them would say yes. However, their dog's performance when asked to sit would vary widely. Almost everyone's dog would sit if the owner held up a full dinner bowl when they were alone in the kitchen, but how many dogs would sit when visitors are arriving and two other dogs are leaping and barking at the door? Ah, there's the rub! The right question isn't does your dog "know" the sit signal, it's how reliable is his response under a variety of circumstances. Professional athletes "know" how to hit a perfect serve or throw a perfect pass, but that doesn't mean they can do it every time they want to.

Our dogs are like that too, so don't fall in the trap of getting angry at your dog because you think he "knows" better. Remember that "knowing" how to do something right doesn't mean that anyone—human or dog—can always do it right, any time, anywhere.

Good dogs are made not born, and they rely on you to be their coaches, cheerleaders and benevolent leaders.

WHAT'S NEXT?

Of course, you're not close to "done" after six weeks of work. Our basic training program at Dog's Best Friend, Ltd. includes six weeks of Beginning Family Dog Training and six weeks of Intermediate class. That's the bare minimum of classes that we recommend for people who want polite, happy family dogs. Don't forget though, that it takes a long time for dogs to learn all the rules of human society and to develop the emotional maturity necessary to be able to follow them. A twelve-week training program is designed to teach you to train your dog. It takes dogs a lot longer to master all that we expect from them. You can make it easier and more fun by taking lots of different types of classes, from Outdoor Intermediate and Advanced classes to Tricks and Games, Tracking, Agility and Competition. You can even learn to teach your dog dance steps and create a special tango for just the two of you. Besides classes, there are some wonderful books and videos that can help you keep training fun for everyone—some of them are listed in the next section to get you started.

And so. . . here's to a long, wonderful life for both you and your dog, and to practicing and playing together to forge the relationship you want. Give your dog a sloppy kiss for putting up with the strange species that we call human, and give yourself a bar of chocolate for your commitment and devotion to your dog. May he grow into the dog of your dreams . . . and never roll in the mud ten minutes before company comes.

RESOURCES

A SELECTION OF TRAINING BOOKS

Aloff, Brenda. 2005. *Canine Body Language: A Photographic Guide.* Wenatchee, Washington: Dogwise.

Aloff, Brenda. 2001. *Positive Reinforcement: Training Dogs in the Real World.* Neptune, NJ: TFH Publications.

Campbell, William E. 1995. *Owner's Guide to Better Behavior in Dogs,* 2nd edition. Loveland, Colorado: Alpine Blue Ribbon Books.

Coren, Stanley. 2000. *How to Speak Dog: Mastering the Art of Dog-Human Communication.* New York: The Free Press.

Coren, Stanley. 2004. *How Dogs Think: Understanding the Canine Mind.* New York: Free Press.

Donaldson, Jean. 1997. *Culture Clash.* Berkeley, California: James and Kenneth Publishers.

Dunbar, Ian. 1998. *How to Teach a New Dog Old Tricks.* Berkeley, California: James and Kenneth Publishers.

Hetts, Suzanne and Estep, Dan. 2000. Video: *Canine Behavior Program: Body Postures and Evaluating Behavioral Health.* Denton, TX: Animal Care Training.

Hunter, Roy. 1995. *Fun Nosework for Dogs.* Eliot, Maine: Howln Moon Press.

King, Trish. 2004. *Parenting Your Dog.* Neptune, NJ: TFH Publications.

McConnell, Patricia. 2002. *The Other End of the Leash: Why We Do What We Do Around Dogs.* New York: Ballantine

Miller, Pat. 2004. *Positive Perspectives: Love Your Dog, Train Your Dog.* Wenatchee, WA: Dogwise.

Pryor, Karen. 2005. *Clicker Training for Dogs.* Waltham, MA: Sunshine Books.

Pryor, Karen. 1985. *Don't Shoot the Dog*. New York: Bantan Books.

Reid, Pamela. 1996. *Excel-erated Learning: Explaining in plain English how dogs learn and how best to teach them*. Oakland, California: James and Kenneth Publishers.

Ryan, Terry. 1998. *The Toolbox for Remodeling Your Problem Dog*. New York: Howell Book House.

Yin, Sophia. 2004. *How to Behave So Your Dog Behaves*. Neptune, NJ: TFH.

MAGAZINES, BOOKS AND VIDEO SOURCES

www.thebark.com Bark: "the modern dog culture magazine," featuring essays, poems, articles and interviews about the relationship of dogs and humans.

www.dogsbestfriendtraining.com A full selection of all of Patricia McConnell's books, booklets, videos and taped seminars, plus information about her speeches and seminars around the country.

www.dogwise.com Dogwise: an online resource, appropriately called "the Amazon of dog books and videos."

www.tawzerdogvideos.com Tawzer Dog Videos has a selection of hundreds of videos related to positive methods of dog training, including videos of seminars by the top trainers and behaviorists in the country.

www.whole-dog-journal.com Whole Dog Journal is a "monthly guide to natural dog care and training" and has lots of excellent articles on alternative medicine and care.

BOOKS ABOUT OUR RELATIONSHIP WITH DOGS

Bark, Editors of. 2003. *Dog is My Co-Pilot: Great Writers on the World's Oldest Friendship*. New York: Crown Publishers.

Clothier, Suzanne. 2005. *Bones Would Rain from the Sky: Deepening our Relationship with Dogs*. Clayton, Victoria, Canada: Warner Books.

Grandin, Temple. 2005. *Animals in Translation: Using the Mysteries of Autism to Decode Animal Behavior*. New York: Scribner.

Grogan, John. 2005. *Marley and Me: Life and Love with the World's Worst Dog*. New York: William Morrow.

Katz, Jon. 2003. *A Dog Year: Twelve Months, Four Dogs, and Me*. New York: Villard.

Knapp, Caroline. 1995. *Pack of Two: The Intricate Bond Between People and Dogs*. New York: Dial Press.

McAuliffe, Claudeen. 2006. *Mindful Dog Teaching: Reflections on the Relationship We Share with our Dogs*. Oconomowoc, WI: Kindness Canine Behavior and Consulting

Yoffe, Emily. 2005. *What the Dog Did: Tales from a formerly reluctant dog owner*. New York: Bloomsbury.

ACKNOWLEDGEMENTS

We have many people to thank for their invaluable feedback and thoughtful readings of earlier drafts. Jim Billings, Ian Dunbar, Trish King, Karen London, Charlie Reinhardt, Susan Michaud, Lorah Marquardt, Sarah Sirios, Denise Swedlund, Julie Vanderloop, and Chelse Wieland stepped up to the plate and added much to the book.

We also thank Becky Addington, Nadia Bidwell, Molly Buchs, Khris Erickson, Harriet Irwin, Susan Michaud, Lisa Milbrandt, Cheryl Osinga, Hope Rutten, Sarah Sirios, Shannon Skolaski, Amy Timm, Julie Vanderloop, Chelse Wieland, and Catherine Young and for their input and efforts in developing the curriculum for our Family Dog Training Classes.

In addition, Patricia gives special thanks to Will (the puppy on the cover and the young nephew of Cool Hand Luke), who has allowed her to road test every line of every page, and to her sweet, old Pippy Tay, the Border Collie who never read the breed description.

Aimee thanks her spirited American Eskimo Dog, Keanu, who brought her into a world she never thought she would enter.